WENSLEYD

Catherine Dinsdale.
Parker

'Wensleydale, Wensleydale, pride of the free,
There's e'er a deep longing to come back to thee.'

Song of Wensleydale

WENSLEYDALE

A David Leather

First published in 1991 by
Smith Settle Ltd
Ilkley Road
Otley
West Yorkshire
LS21 3JP

ISBN 1 870071 71 9

Designed, printed and bound by
SMITH SETTLE
Ilkley Road, Otley, West Yorkshire LS21 3JP

CONTENTS

For Kevin, whose advice I took.

INTRODUCTION

Walking is now the most popular form of exercise, and what better way is there of exploring the countryside at the same time? This guide for walkers is packed with information which brings the scenery of Wensleydale to life.

The plan for this new and original style of walking book came from Smith Settle Ltd. It is a combination of the 'go-over-the-stile-and-diagonally-across-the-field' approach, with that of the nature or history trail, where points of interest are described as you go along. The result not only draws attention to birds, animals and plants that are likely to be seen on each walk, together with interesting facts about the different species, but also explains the geology and scenery, and explores the history of the dale, its customs and folkore.

Four introductory chapters relate specifically to Wensleydale by describing its landscape, history and wildlife, and the book has a bibliography for more detailed reading, and a useful index which helps to quickly pinpoint a favourite topic.

There are twenty-one beautiful walks, ranging from a short three miles (5km) to a full day's hike of fourteen miles (22km). All start and finish at the same place, usually in a village where there is parking or public transport available, and a summary of the public transport services is given. Each walk has a short introductory paragraph, which details any difficult conditions, though a good pair of walking boots and waterproofs are always advisable. Directions are kept to a minimum and tend to be at the beginning of each paragraph. More detailed directions are given where it is easy to miss the way. The time given for each walk does not allow time for stops, picnics or photography, so, if you are out for the day, add about a third to the stated walking time. The description of each walk draws attention to all kinds of things to look out for and find along the way, but there is lots left to discover for yourself, using the background provided by the introductory chapters.

This is a personal selection of walks, which are by no means official routes. Although great care has been taken to follow rights of way, these often change in small ways. Additions and modifications are made from time to time, often to the benefit of walkers. Where a section of the route occasionally departs from a recognised right of way, mention is made of it.

The photographs, line drawings and watercolours are so placed that they illustrate points described in the text. Jeremy Taylor has done a great job on the beautifully executed drawings and watercolours, and Janet Rawlins has provided some of her stunning paintings of flowers along with some line drawings. Jim Jarratt provided the diagram of drystone walls. The excellent photographs are by Trevor Croucher, and the author. Additional illustrations are also by the author.

Large, clear maps by the author for each of the walks show the route and the adjacent features, which should be suffcient to find the way, though you may like to make use of the appropriate Ordnance Survey 1:25,000 Outdoor Leisure map (2½ inches to the mile) to identify distant views. The smaller scale Landranger maps at 1:50,000 are also useful in relating the walk to the surrounding area. In using the grid references given at the beginning of each walk, don't forget to read first from the foot (or top) of the map.

It requires some concentration to train oneself to see and hear signs of the natural world, and to develop a 'seeing eye' in an appreciation of what lies behind the scenery and what the landscape can reveal. It takes practice to listen for bird songs, to spot flowers or to interpret the shape of the land, but the knowledge gained adds a great deal to the appreciation of the environment and provides much personal satisfaction.

When you are out walking, take back with you happy memories, notes, sketches or photographs, but please leave undisturbed the wild flowers, rocks and fossils for the enjoyment of others. Remember to follow the Country Code, and respect the life and work of the countryside.

I would like to thank Professor Cuchlaine King for her generous help on the geomorphology of Wensleydale, Ian Hunter for information on the discovery of fossil footprints, Keith Good for his help on birds, Deborah Millward for allowing me to draw freely from her book *A Flora of Wensleydale*, and Jean Pollard for the route to walk 3 and her knowledge of local history. I would like particularly to thank Mark Whitley of Smith Settle Ltd, who has given so much guidance and encouragement in the production of this book.

A D Leather
Ilkley 1991

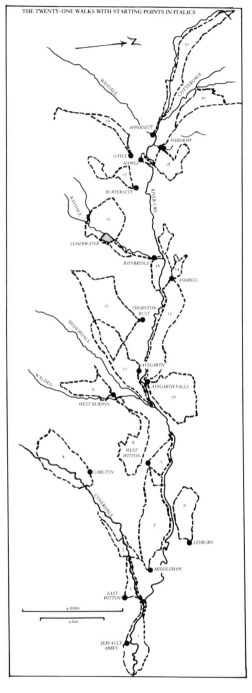

THE TWENTY-ONE WALKS WITH STARTING POINTS IN ITALICS

ix

ASKRIGG
722'
220 m

The starting point of each walk is given in bold print with altitude in both feet and metres

route and way round

other paths

streams and rivers with direction of flow

crags and scars

1378'
420 m

1000'
305 m

spot heights have altitude in feet and metres above sea level

Y.H.

selected camp sites, churches, car parks and Youth Hostels

KEY TO MAPS

PUBLIC TRANSPORT

The nearest British Rail passenger stations are Garsdale Head on the Settle-Carlisle line, with a daily bus service into Hawes, and Northallerton Station which has bus connections to Leyburn.

United Services and Postbus run between Leyburn and Hawes via Aysgarth and via Askrigg. Care is needed when planning, as times vary on different days of the week and between winter and summer. In the summer there is also the Dalesbus which runs at weekends. An excellent and comprehensive timetable entitled *Dales Connections* gives all these bus services with rail connections. It is free of charge from United Automobile Services Ltd , Grange Road, Darlington, Co Durham (0325 468771). The latest editions should be available from Tourist Information and National Park Centres at Leyburn (0969 23069), Hawes (0969 667450), and Aysgarth Falls (0969 663424).

ROCKS AND THE LANDSCAPE

The lovely valley of Wensleydale is broader than the other Yorkshire Dales. It also has more villages, richer farmland and more side valleys. Charles Kingsley referred to it as 'the richest spot in all England', and John Wesley wrote in his journal for 1st May 1790:

'Loveley Wensleydale, the largest by far of all the Dales and the most beautiful.'

It starts high in the Pennines, where the valley is more open and exposed, but further down it is clothed with walls and hedges, woods and meadows in a distinctly park-like, pastoral scenery. When compared with Wharfedale its surrounding hills are not as high or steep, yet it has many waterfalls and fast-flowing streams. It is a dale of almost flat-topped hills and horizontal scars and terraces, of numerous hillocks on the valley floor and a large natural lake, of limestones and flagstones and distant views. Being further from population centres it is quieter and has fewer visitors than Wharfedale, and on many of the footpaths you are unlikely to meet another person.

Wensleydale is the exception in not being named after its river, for it is the River Ure that drains the dale. In fact the old name of Yoredale (or Uredale) persisted alongside that of Wensleydale until the beginning of the eighteenth century, and the geologist John Philips used it to name the rocks which he first studied there. For 100 years, from 1202, Wensley was the only market town in the dale and continued to be of importance until the middle of the sixteenth century.

Although the River Ure has its source high on the side of Lunds Fell, on the borders of Cumbria, the valley of Wensleydale really begins at the Moorcock Inn. The riverbed here lies 1,000 feet (305m) above sea level, and from the Moorcock to Kilgram Bridge at the lower end of the dale, a distance of twenty-six miles (41½ km), the river drops 705 feet (215m) in height to just under 300 feet (90m) above sea level. About a third of this fall comes in the three miles (5km) between Aysgarth and Redmire with the series of waterfalls.

The best way to experience the delights of the landscape is by walking, to inspect it at close quarters, to see the subtle changes of colour, to hear the sounds of falling water or the call of the first curlew, or to catch the scent of spring blossom or of a freshly-cut meadow. In Wensleydale, it is the smaller-scale beauty that attracts, and an understanding of what lies behind the scenery, its rocks, people, wildlife, trees and flowers all add to a greater appreciation of its charm.

Wensleydale Granite The natural landscape often depends on the types of rock and how they lie near the surface. In Wensleydale one can go a step further and say that the scenery is strongly influenced by a deep structure one third of a mile below ground. For, 1,640 feet (500m) below the surface, lies a mass of beautiful pink granite! The museum at Hawes has a piece of this handsome rock, a length of core from the borehole which was drilled in Raydale above Semerwater in the summer of 1973. Until then geologists had only predicted the probable presence of granite, but no man had set eyes on it until that unique moment, when it was proved beyond doubt. The colour of the rock is a pale mottle of salmon pink, white and tinges of green, and tests have shown its age to be about 400 million years old.

This large granite mass has had three major influences on Wensleydale's land-

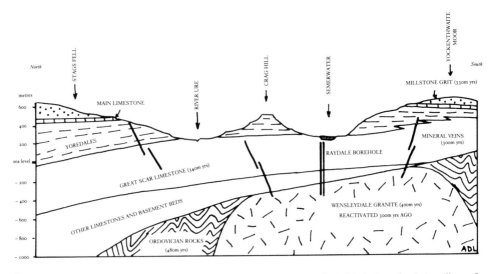

Section to show the position of the Wensleydale granite. Length of section ten miles (16 km). Ages of rocks in millions of years.

scape. To begin with, the granite forms a rigid platform for the flat-lying limestones and sandstones which sit on it. The result can be seen in the many horizontal scars and terraces on the valley sides, and in the lack of any folds in the strata. Secondly, the granite is a relatively lightweight rock and this has given an uplift to the region to form a large area of high ground. The same buoyancy led to massive erosion of the overlying coal measures which once lay on top of the present strata. A third influence is that about 300 million years ago, after all the Carboniferous rocks had been laid down, the granite became hot again and pushed upwards slightly, causing many cracks or faults in the overlying strata. Along these cracks, hot fluids pushed their way, to cool and crystallise as lead ore, calcite, fluorite, barite and other minerals.

Lower Carboniferous Rocks The Great Scar limestone was deposited first,

on the eroded surface of the granite, starting about 350 million years ago. Only the top of this thick limestone is visible today along the floor of the valley of Wensleydale. It extends from Aysgarth upstream as far as Appersett. It also occurs in Raydale and Bishopdale, but for the most part is covered over by glacial deposits.

The Yoredales consist of a repeated series of rocks, a sandwich with a limestone first, a shale in the middle and a sandstone on the top. The change of rock type reflects the change in environment at the time of deposition. A limestone indicates a warm, clear sea with no sediment from any land and plenty of marine life; shale shows that mud reached the area probably from a large delta spreading out from the north; and sandstone represents sandbanks on the delta top. Because the delta was being fed by rivers from the north, as it thrust south into the shallow sea, the coarser sands were

2

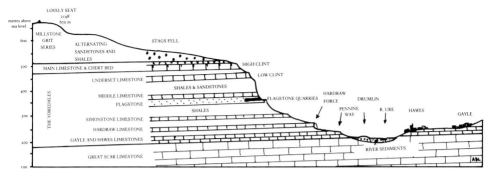

Geological section from Lovely Seat to Gayle to show details of the Yoredales. Length of section four miles (6½ km).

not carried so far, and are much thinner towards the south. In Wharfedale, for example, Yoredale sandstones are rare and thin. At Askrigg the total thickness of the Yoredales is 900 feet (275m); this shrinks to 575 feet (175m) further south on Fountains Fell and thickens to 1,300 feet (400m) to the north at Kirkby Stephen. Sometimes the delta built up above sea level, and primitive rain forests grew amid the lagoons and meandering river channels. Early amphibians lived in these swamps and the footprints of a crocodile-like creature have been found at Hardraw Force (*walk 18*).

The great Yorkshire geologist John Phillips examined these rocks and published his description of them as long ago as 1836. He used the name 'Yoredale' for his 'type area' for this group of strata. Phillips appreciated the repetitive nature of the rocks and understood the changes from north to south:

'. . . variable inundations from the land and inconstant movements near the shores of the sea.'

The whole region at the time of deposition was likely to have been rather flat, so that a small increase in sea level or a slight uplift of the land would have had far-reaching effects on what was being deposited where, on the sea floor. The sandwich of limestone, shale and sandstone is repeated eight times, each being known by the name of its limestone. Many of the names Phillips gave them are still in use, such as the Hawes and Hardraw limestones. The Hardraw limestone forms a prominent step along the sides of the dale, outcropping at Hardraw Force and Mill Gill Force, and, on the south side, the village of Thornton Rust is built on it.

Upper Carboniferous Rocks Great thicknesses of millstone grit and coal measure strata, up to a mile thick (1,600m), have been eroded away through geological time due to the uplifting effect of the granite. Today only a thin veneer of Upper Carboniferous rocks remains. These include the seventy foot (22m) thick Main limestone which, although it looks like another Yoredale limestone, officially comes in the lower part of the Upper Carboniferous. This is because of its age as dated by fossils. It forms very prominent, high scars such as Ellerkin Scar near Askrigg and High Clint near Hardraw. In places it contains masses of crinoid stems and *Gigantoproductus* shells. On top of the Main limestone is a bed of chert mixed with limestone. Chert is a flinty rock, entirely

3

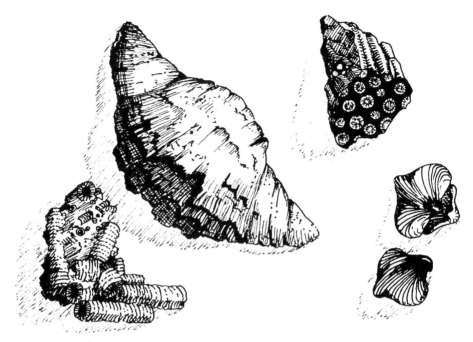

Limestone fossils (left to right): crinoid stems, gigantoproductus, lithostrotion and small brachiopods.

made up of silica. It has been quarried for use in the ceramic industry at Flint Hill on Wether Fell.

The Millstone Grit series consists of coarse, pebbly gritstones with shale bands. They outcrop on the tops of the fells as on Dodd Fell, Penhill, Great Haw and a small patch on Wether Fell, and more widely on Great Shunner Fell to the north. Coal seams have been worked in places, as on the sides of Great Shunner Fell (*walk 20*). The millstone grit is the youngest rock in the area, being about 330 million years old. A lot of the gritstone is covered with peat and acid soils which have a marked effect on the vegetation.

Limestone Scenery The Yoredale limestones are too thin to develop the typical scenery of limestone country. However, the alternating limestones, shales and sandstones have produced a very special sort of landscape in Wensleydale. The shales weather easily, and the harder limestones jut out as almost horizontal steps and scars on the valley sides or as cappings to the flat-topped hills. The Underset limestone forms Ivy Scar, and the plateau-like Crag Hill and Wether Fell are topped by the Main limestone. There are numerous sink holes and swallow holes on the upper surface of the limestone, and springs lower down where streamlets reappear at its foot. Highly acid water from the peat moors has a striking effect on limestone, producing a scalloped surface as it dissolves it away. Swallow holes and springs occur widely around Wether Fell

Ellerkin Scar above Askrigg, an outcrop of the Main limestone.

and above Thornton Rust. Wide areas of limestone pavements are rare in Wensleydale.

The Ice Age The last time the ice advanced in Britain was between 25,000 and 15,000 years ago. The Dales had its own ice cap, centred on Great Shunner Fell and Wild Boar Fell, and ice ground its way down the valleys. Bishopdale (*walks 11 and 13*) contained a steep and active glacier, which eroded a deep U-shaped valley, so deep that the valley is lower than Wensleydale, into which it drains. Walden (*walk 9*), in contrast, led a sheltered existence and its V-shaped profile shows that it suffered

little or no erosion by the ice. In the wider valley of Wensleydale the glacier was slow-moving and so had less erosive power. The valley sides were scoured to establish the present stepped appearance, but most important of all are the deposits left behind by the ice.

The glacial deposits of Wensleydale distinguish it from the other dales. They include drift tails, drumlins and moraines, which are described by Professor Cuchlaine King in her book on the geomorphology of Northern England. Drift tails are generally rather rare and unusual features, and there are many very good examples here. They formed at the junction of tributary valleys and are made up of glacial till (a mixture of boulders, sand and clay). You can see them joined to the spurs of rock at the branch valleys. They form long tails pointing downstream, are often moulded into rounded drumlin-like shapes and tend to divert the incoming streams further to the east. This deflection of tributaries is largely responsible for many of the waterfalls on the side streams. A drift tail diverts Cotterdale Beck and helps create Cotter Force and, further along, Fossdale Gill is deflected over Hardraw Force and round the drift tail. There is a large drift tail between Bishopdale and Wensleydale.

Drumlins are long, rounded hills shaped under the ice. At the head of the dale between Hell Gill and the Moorcock Inn there are several of these smooth oval mounds. There are more between Bainbridge and Aysgarth on both sides of the river, and one of them is Brough Hill with the Roman fort on top. This measures half a mile (800m) long and 100 feet (30m) high. Lady Hill, with its crown of pine trees, is a special example, as it is mainly solid rock but still shaped by the ice. The best one is between Askrigg and Bainbridge (*walk 16*), its till having been exposed by the River Ure which flows on its southern side. Drumlins are steeper at the upstream end, and in shape resemble an egg cut lengthways.

Moraines are also formed of till, but are often less clayey than drumlins and drift tails, since they were formed at the sides or at the snout of the glacier, where there was likely to be more water, washing out some of the clay. Lateral moraines occur on both sides of the river near Aysgarth and Bainbridge. At Aysgarth there is a conspicuous terminal moraine, and another crosses the valley floor at Brown Moor almost two miles (3km) below Hawes. Both of these created dams across the valley floor

and held up shallow lakes for a time; these now form river flood plains, one above Aysgarth extending almost to Bainbridge and the other around Hawes.

Semerwater Natural lakes are rare in Yorkshire and Semerwater (*walk 15*) is one of the larger ones. Its origin is also glacial. It was dammed at its lower end by glacial debris and the lake formerly was much bigger, stretching further up Raydale, an area above the present lake which is now flat and rather marshy. The overflow from this glacial lake formed the gorge and falls of the River Bain above Bainbridge. The former course of the Bain at the Countersett end is blocked by a drift tail. Crooks Beck, which enters Semerwater, is still helping to fill in the lake with silt and mud and has formed a small delta at the south-west corner.

Waterfalls There are many beautiful waterfalls in Wensleydale, both on the side streams and on the Ure itself. The hard beds of limestone and sandstone with softer shales beneath provide the perfect situation. The waterfalls wear backwards upstream, leaving gorges below them. Hardraw (*walk 18*) is the highest single drop fall in England (90ft or 27m), and a visit to it provides a clear explanation of how a waterfall is formed. The hard bed on the top is sandstone, overlain by the Hardraw limestone, and thick shales can be seen behind the falls. The wearing back of the waterfall has formed a gorge nearly 1,000 feet (300m) long. If the fall originated 15,000 years ago, when the ice melted from this area, then it has retreated on average by three-quarters of an inch (2cm) per year. Of similar origin are the impressive falls of Mill Gill Force and Whitfield Force (*walk 14*) near Askrigg.

The spectacular waterfalls at Aysgarth are one of the most popular attractions in the dale and consist of three separate falls, with the whole of the River Ure cascading over them. Not of glacial origin but formed due to a rise in the level of the land, they are cut in thick limestones separated by thin shales which produces the stepped formations. A little further down river is the less widely-known Redmire Force which can only be reached on foot (*walk 7*). The Ure is very impressive after heavy rain, when the peat-stained river surges thunderously down the waterfalls. Cotter Force is shrouded in a woodland setting where the waters of Cotterdale Beck splash over a series of limestone steps. At Gayle the thinly-bedded limestones provide a staircase of waterfalls rather like those at Bainbridge. West Burton has its own lovely falls, and another pretty one is on Widdale Beck just below Appersett viaduct. There are many more on the side streams to discover for yourself and each one is unique in pattern and beauty.

MAN AND THE LANDSCAPE

Early Settlers The wide and welcoming valley of Wensleydale had plenty of space for prehistoric peoples. The limestone terraces, which were less thickly wooded and better drained than the valley floor, made perfect inroads and homes for early settlers. The first to make their mark (from about 4,000 BC) were the Neolithic or New Stone Age people. They were the first cultivators and must have been well-organised to construct the large henges like the one at Castle Dykes near Aysgarth (*walk 11*). This ceremonial site was probably still in use into the Bronze Age.

Bronze Age settlers arrived about 2,000 BC, bringing the use of metal and pottery for the first time, though still working flint. They built stone circles like the one on Oxclose pasture near Carperby (*walk 12*). In the late Bronze Age and early Iron Age, settled farms were established and the remains of hut circles and small fields can be seen at Tullis Cote above Wensley (*walk 6*) and on the south side of Addlebrough (*walk 13*). The remains of a village on stilts have been found in the shallows of Semerwater which may date back to the Neolithic period.

The Brigantes arrived in the third century BC with horses and chariots, beautiful metalwork and pottery. These Celtic peoples had a good system of farming, enclosing fields and growing barley, wheat and peas. They made small, hand grindstones known as querns, and their way of farming probably continued for hundreds of years until the Angles and Danes arrived. Communities settled high on Penhill and Addlebrough.

The Romans When the Romans came, the Brigantes, under Venutius, offered fierce resistance by building the great fortress at Stanwick just north of Richmond and a series of smaller forts, including one on Addlebrough. One Roman writer described the Brigantes as 'war-mad, high-spirited and quick for battle', and they proved the most difficult of the tribal groups to conquer. The Romans broke the power of the Brigantes at Stanwick in about AD 74, and constructed military highways into the dale. They built a fort on Brough Hill at Bainbridge, called Virosidum, where up to 500 men were stationed by the commander Agricola. The fort was connected by the straight Roman road, now Cam High Road, across the fells via Ingleton to the Roman base at Ribchester on the Ribble. The Bainbridge fort was attacked more than once by the native British, but was rebuilt and occupied until the fourth century AD. It is still one of the best preserved of Pennine forts, though not at present open to the public.

Angles, Danes and Norse In the seventh century the Angles came into the lower part of Wensleydale – the place names ton, ley and ham show the distribuion. Places with these endings, like Witton, Bolton, Wensley, Braidley, Middleham and Coverham, are common below Askrigg. These people had a well-organised communal system, living in small villages and farming the land round about. Crop land was ploughed in strips, groups of which are known as a furlong.

Two centuries later the Danes settled in parts of the main dale and in some of the smaller dales, leaving the place name elements by (farmstead) and thorp (outlying hamlet) in Thoralby, Carberby and Agglethorpe. In the middle of the tenth century, Norse Vikings came from the west into the head of Wensleydale. They were independent pastoral farmers, used to life in the Scandinavian mountains, who moved sheep between winter and summer pastures – the 'saetr', which becomes *sett* in Appersett, Burtersett and Countersett, the ABC of Wensleydale; *thwaite* has the meaning of a sloping clearing in a wooded area, as in Braithwaite and Swinithwaite.

Norman Castles When the Norman conquerers arrived they set aside large parts of Wensleydale as hunting forests, and about the year 1070 wiped out much of the local population in the'Harrying of the North'. The *Domesday Book* records many villages as 'waste', but there is no reference to any place in Wensleydale above Askrigg. This was woodland reserved for the Norman passion of hunting, though the Norse farms were allowed to continue raising a few fenced-in cattle and pigs in return for looking after the deer. Those who lived there were under strict forest law with no hunting, cutting of timber or clearing of undergrowth. The lords of Middleham hunted Wensleydale and Bishopdale. Bainbridge was built for twelve foresters under a Norman forest warden, and each forester had a house and two acres of land.

The Normans built castles to establish their authority and an early timbered one was erected by Ribald on William's Hill at Middleham (*walk 3*), a circular mound surrounded by a ditch and bank. The massive castle nearby was started about 1170 by Ribald's grandson, Robert Fitz Randolph. It was Randolph's daughter Mary who brought the manor into the ownership of the most powerful family in England by her marriage to Lord Robert Neville. The Nevilles ruled at Middleham for nearly 300 years, producing many great men until the greatest of them all, Richard Neville, Earl of Warwick, 'the Kingmaker' and last of the feudal barons, made the castle his home.

These were the great years in the history of the town. Harry Speight in his book *Romantic Richmondshire* describes the Middleham of those heady days:

'Few places have such distinguished heritages as Middleham, few have such high-placed chiefs and heroes, have witnessed such pomp and magnificence, such scenes of revelry, such princely festivities, such gorgeous retinues as this "Windsor of the North", during that eventful era of the strife between the White Rose and the Red.'

Warwick was killed in 1471 in the Wars of the Roses and Middleham was bestowed on Richard, Duke of Gloucester. The boy Richard had come to live at Middleham when he was eleven to train to be a knight and be educated. His friends were Robert Percy, Francis Lovell, and the girls Isabel and Anne Neville. Ten years later in 1472 he married Anne, his boyhood sweetheart, and their only son Prince Edward was born in the castle. The couple stayed at Middleham, their favourite home, for eleven years until Richard of Gloucester became King Richard III. Their son Edward died suddenly at the age of eleven and Richard was later slain at the Battle of Bosworth in 1485.

The Abbeys of Jervaulx and Coverham
The monasteries had a great effect on both lives and landscape. In a period of religious enthusiasm, Norman lords were generous in giving land to various orders – these gifts ensured for them a place in Heaven. In 1156, Cistercian monks founded Jervaulx Abbey (*walk 1*) after moving from Fors near Askrigg (*walk 16*), and the abbey at Coverham (*walk 3*) was established by the Premonstratensians in 1212 after having moved from Swainby on the Swale. Jervaulx became very wealthy, owning much of the lower dale and land on the north side of the river above Askrigg,

known now as Abbotside. Outlying 'granges' or working farms such as those at Braithwaite and Grange were established to manage the huge estates.

Wool from the great flocks of sheep was the main wealth but, over a long period, sheep grazing had a profound effect on the landscape. Sheep will eat all tree seedlings, so any open woodland or scattered trees died of old age with no young trees to replace them. The result was the formation of wide-open stretches of rough grazing land, now a familiar part of the scenery.

Villages and Markets For over 300 years from about 1200 AD, Wensleydale was part hunting and part monastic estate, and the castles and abbeys both gave rise to trade and markets. Castles needed food and clothing, and abbeys had wool to sell. But these were also hard times, with raids by the Scots and regular outbreaks of plague. Wensley was an important market town in medieval times, giving its name to the whole valley, but suffered terribly from plague in 1563 when many died and others fled the town. Askrigg had developed on the edge of the forest and took over as the chief market town until the end of the eighteenth century, when Hawes grew rapidly. Middleham reaped the benefits of the presence of the castle and the Nevilles, and has continued as a small market town for 600 years since its market charter was granted in 1387.

Small terraces or lynchets developed in the late medieval period. These are beautifully preserved near Askrigg (*walk 16*) and Carperby. The plough cut into the hillside, turning the earth in the easier downhill direction, while the stones turned up by the plough were placed on the steep slope bordering the next strip. The terraces are a natural result of many years of this type of farming.

Villages mentioned in the *Domesday Book*

The medieval farming system: lynchets near Askrigg.

include the lost village of Thoresby (*walk 10*), and West Scrafton, Caldbergh and Carlton, in Coverdale, all now rather unimportant hamlets. Preston-under-Scar, Redmire and Castle Bolton are three more 'Domesday' villages which found the railway an advantage, but are now served only by minor roads. Leyburn, on the other hand, was a small village for hundreds of years and only grew into Wensleydale's main market town in the nineteenth century. Bainbridge, in spite of its Roman fort, was only a forest lodge by Norman times. Its subsequent position on a crossing of drove roads and turnpike was more favourable to its growth.

Manor Houses Bolton Castle dominates the northern slopes of the Wensleydale, its massive structure visible from miles around. This is the supreme example of the fortified manor house and is the best-preserved medieval castle in the country. Built for Richard Scrope, chancellor to Richard II, it took eighteen years to build, cost £12,000 and was completed in 1399. It had four corner towers each almost 100 feet (30m) high. The Scropes were a powerful family: Richard Scrope fought at

Lunds Church is probably late seventeenth century, and its simplicity suggests it was built by its parishioners.

Crecy and many other battles, a Lord Scrope fought against the Scots at Flodden Field, Henry Scrope appears in Shakespeare's *Henry V*, and for six months from July 1568 another Henry Scrope had charge of Mary Queen of Scots, who had fled from Scotland hoping for help from Queen Elizabeth. In 1656, during the Civil War, the castle was under siege by Cromwell's forces and those within were starved into submission. The north-east tower was badly hit by cannon fire and fell down during storms over a century later.

The castle (*walk 10*) is now a museum, and you can see the apartment and bed which Mary used. The dungeon, armourer's forge, ale house and threshing floor have been brought to life again for visitors. The view from the roof is magnificent.

Henry VIII's dissolution of the monas-teries may have brought wealth to the king, but only difficult times came for the ordinary people. They had always relied on these religious institutions for selling their produce, for employment and as centres of learning and healing. Adam Sedbergh, the Abbot of Jervaulx, joined the rebellion of the Pilgrimage of Grace, hiding on Witton Fell for four days, but this only led to savage reprisals, misery and the eventual hanging of the abbot.

Wealthy landowners did benefit from the breakup of the monastic estates. Coleby Hall near Askrigg is a Tudor manor house, and two miles (3km) down the dale is the castellated Nappa Hall, the home of the influential Metcalfes. The Scropes' Danby Hall (*walk 1*) is near Middleham and Braithwaite Hall (*walk 3*), now owned by the National Trust, is on the other side of the river. In time, many tenant farmers on these estates purchased their own land to become yeoman farmers.

Farms, Barns, Walls and Bridges

By the end of the seventeenth century there were more peaceful and prosperous times. Stone houses and farms were being built throughout the dale. Gritstone was the most easily worked building stone, and in limestone areas a house had limestone walls and gritstone cornerstones and lintels. The traditional Dales house has a simple design, built with the weather in mind. The buildings invariably face south to get as much advantage from the sun as possible, with few windows on the north and west sides. The walls are thick and the low-angle roofs are stone-slated. One of the oldest farmhouses in the dale is Worton Hall (*walk 16*), dated 1600. Its long, low profile is typical, with stone slate roof and stone mullioned windows. Doorways are a feature of Dales architecture, built from large blocks of gritstone. The lintels are often carved and decorated with interesting designs, with the date and initials of the couple who first lived in the house. One near the market cross in Askrigg is inscribed 'FTA 1687'.

Farming went through its own revolution. The enclosing of fields by stone walls ensured careful breeding of animals, and improved production was achieved by new farming methods of, for example, the draining of boggy land, liming and manuring. The hillsides are dotted with limekilns, in which limestone and coal or timber were burnt to produce lime to 'sweeten' the fields, as well as for mortar for building. Field barns could each house four or five cows through the winter, fed on the hay stored in the loft above. Small, irregular field walls had already been built near to villages, but following an Act of Parliament all land had to be enclosed. The better-off,

landowning yeoman farmers did well out of the enclosures, but the poorer farmers lost their right to graze animals as the common land was taken over, and they either became farm-labourers or found work in the towns. The many miles of stone walls were built mainly between 1780 and 1820, and so average nearly 200 years old. Drove roads and packhorse routes were preserved, as the winding green lanes we know today, and footpaths had stiles built for them. The field barns, limekilns and drystone walls were to become a much-loved part of the dale's scenery.

The many elegant stone bridges are an outstanding feature of Wensleydale and have survived centuries of wear and tear and surging floodwaters. Aysgarth Bridge (*walk 12*) has been widened but the large single arch, originally only about nine feet (2.75m) in width, may date from about 1640, after the existing one was reported in ruins. Another beautiful single span is the pointed arch of Coverham Abbey Bridge (*walk 3*) which had repairs made to it in 1615 and 1659, and most likely erected by the monks of Coverham. Two of the pointed arches in Wensley Bridge may go back to the end of the fourteenth century, and Leland in the 1540s described this as the 'great bridge of stone'. The massive bridge at Ulshaw (*walk 1*) has four arches and a sundial on it dated 1674, which may have been the date of a major repair. The six huge cut-waters are very impressive and the recesses are useful for walkers as the road is only twelve feet (3.65m) between parapets. Kilgram Bridge (*walk 1*) could be fifteenth century and it is possible that the six arches are the original structure. In 1748 during the terrible cattle plague, the bridge was watched by two men day and night to avoid movement of cattle.

Droving

The growth of the urban population in England and the breeding of

Wensley Bridge. Note the differently-shaped arches.

cattle in the Highlands of Scotland led to a big cattle trade between north and south. Meat was needed in the towns, and drovers brought cattle and sheep in their thousands from fairs near the Scottish border, south along the drove roads and into the Yorkshire Dales. Fairs such as those at Middleham Moor and Askrigg did well out of this trade, and Middleham Fair even issued its own £5 notes with illustrations of local beauty spots. One of the main routes to Ingleton followed the Roman road from Askrigg, through Bainbridge, and over Wether Fell and Cam Fell via Ribble Head. Another went down the dale to Middleham and Masham. Progress was slow, perhaps twelve miles a day, with four drovers in charge of herds of up to 200 cattle and 2,000 sheep. Cows were often given iron shoes because of the long distances they had to travel, some of them being sold in the Midlands or London.

Small Industries and other Occupations Wool was still the most important commodity, and spinning and knitting became a cottage industry in every village. Men, women and children all took their part knitting caps, gloves, jerseys and stockings, specialising in items for seamen. Hawes and Gayle developed as the centres for this hand-knitting trade, with markets in Richmond and Kendal. Askrigg became well-known for its clock-making and in the eighteenth century was the main centre for the Dales. Mark Metcalfe and Christopher Caygill were early clockmakers, while James Pratt and John Skidmore came later. The clock mechanisms were all made by hand and an eight day grandfather clock cost £5.

Stone-wallers were poor but skilled workers, and a good waller would build seven yards of wall in a day with the help of a boy to put in the fillings. It was a tradition

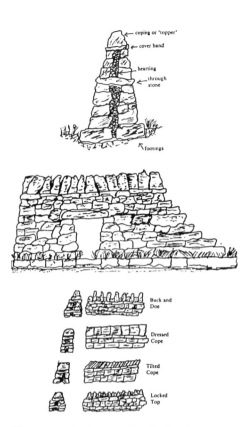

The structure of a drystone wall, with cripple hole, and different types of coping.

A long line of winning racehorses trace their ancestry back to this one horse and many trainers became wealthy owners, Middleham being the main centre.

Mining and Quarrying Although there were many small mines, leadmining was not a big concern in Wensleydale, as it was in the other dales. There were minor workings in Bishopdale, including one at West Burton, with bigger ones in Apedale and Woodhall (*walk 12*).

Local coal was always in demand and preferable to peat, particularly for lead smelting and also in the limekilns. Thin seams occur in the upper part of the Yoredale rocks and in the millstone grit. The spoil heaps of black shale, often grown over, can be seen above Cotterdale (*walk 20*) and at Fossdale Moss on the east side of Great Shunner Fell. The coal was mined by adits – tunnels straight into the hillside – or by bell pits, where a vertical shaft was made to the coal seam, perhaps fifty feet (15m) below the surface. The coal seam, maybe two feet thick (0.6m), was mined in all directions until it became unsafe, then another pit was started. There are several of these old bell pits on the shoulder of Shunner Fell, crossed by the Pennine Way.

Wensleydale was especially noted for its roofing slate, a strong, thinly-bedded sandstone which splits easily. Thin slabs were used for roofing and thicker ones for flooring and paving. Many of the quarries have tunnels into the hillside, as near Carperby (*walk 12*), at Burtersett (*walk 17*) and on the side of Stags Fell (*walk 18*). The flagstone was actually mined in large blocks, then split into flags.

Leisure Wensleydale is great walking country. It has hundreds of miles of footpaths and bridleways with a tremendous variety of surroundings from wooded riverside to wild mountain fell, from

that when the waller arrived at the wall in the morning he would throw the heaviest hammer up the hillside and that would be the length of wall to be built that day. Drainers were another poor group of workers who did their work under contract. They had to work all the hours of daylight, living on the plainest food of oatcake and cheese. Lower down the dale, horse breeding took on a new meaning when an Arabian stallion was brought into the area.

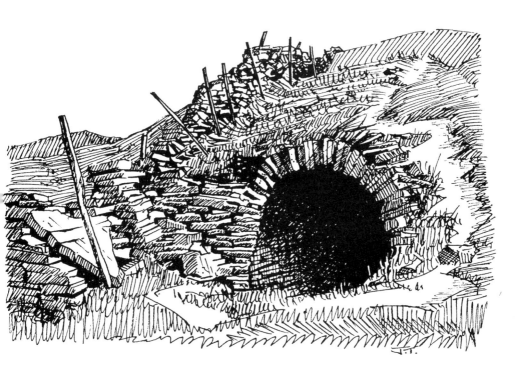

A mine for roofing slate on Stags Fell.

flowery limestone scars to dark peat bogs. The Yoredale Way, established by Ken Piggin, is a 100 mile (160km) long-distance footpath from York to Kirkby Stephen which follows the course of the River Ure along the length of Wensleydale. Nature trails include one in Freeholders Wood at Aysgarth Falls and one at Hardraw Force. There is fishing in the Ure and on Semerwater, hunting of fox and hare on the edge of the fells, and shooting of grouse and pheasant in the season. Cycling is as popular as ever, horse-riding and para-gliding are possible for those enthusiasts, with wind-surfing on Semerwater. There are National Park visitor centres at Hawes and Aysgarth Falls and a wonderful selection of villages and attractions for the most discerning tourist.

WILDLIFE

The rich landscape of Wensleydale is a haven for a plentiful wildlife. There are many habitats that harbour a large number of birds, mammals, butterflies and other interesting creatures. Rushing becks and waterfalls along the tributary valleys, small patches of broadleaved woodland, acres of wild moorland on both sides of the dale, steep crags, lush meadows on the valley floor and a wide expanse of farmland all provide a great variety of places for birds and animals to live. For the walker there is usually something to see, some little surprise round the next corner, whether off the beaten track or close to a busy road or village. If you keep alert to the movements and sounds of your surroundings, it is amazing what you come across.

As for the birdlife, knowing what to expect is half the battle in identification, as most birds keep to their own particular habitat. If the habitat is right, then there you are likely to find the bird. After the simple matter of identification there is always more to find out about behaviour, lifestyle, habits and movements; and many of these things you can discover for yourself by careful observation.

Here are some of the main habitats and the wildlife you may expect to see:

Moorland The wide expanse of high moors bordering the dale can be reached on many of the walks and, although often cold, wet and windswept, there are several birds which make it their home, though few

Golden plover.

remain there in the winter months. The handsome golden plover is spectacular and common enough to be almost Wensleydale's own. On the tops of Great Shunner Fell, Stags Fell and Penhill (*walks 20, 18 and 9*) you will find this beautiful bird with its gold-flecked back and its white-bordered, black breast. In spite of its striking summer plumage, it is well-camouflaged and secretive, but will probably give its position away by its mournful fluting call. Flocks of golden plover of a hundred or more are not uncommon.

The rarer dunlin, known as the 'plover's page', nests in similar terrain, often near standing water. The displaying song flight of the male as it rises and hovers is a magical sound on a still evening. An even smaller bird to brave the bleak and wet landscape is the meadow pipit. This is the most common bird of the rough grassland, the heather and the peat bogs. It spends a lot of time running about looking for insects on the ground, but the display flight of the male is fun to observe, as it rises steeply into the air then parachutes slowly down, delivering a cheerful trill, with fluttering wings and tail up. The skylark returns to the hills by February and entertains with its thrilling, non-stop, high-speed song. It may be that these birds of the treeless moors have developed this kind of aerial song flight because of the lack of a high perch from which to display.

The elegant curlew is our largest wader and its bubbling call delights everyone that hears it. Most are to be seen well below the highest summits, and some take up nest-sites along the river, but the curlew is perhaps the noisiest of the moorland birds. The red grouse lives where heather grows well, as it depends on the green shoots for its food. These game birds tend to remain hidden until you are quite close and then they will explode into the air in a flurry of wing beats, calling 'goback, goback, bak,

bak'. The ring ouzel is fairly common on the higher ground and likes to be near some running water or a rocky outcrop, where it will perch and call 'be quick, be quick, be quick'.

The kestrel is abundant in Wensleydale, and is as much at home on the moors as lower down in the valley. Its old name of windhover describes exactly this bird's characteristic posture of effortlessly hovering into the wind, while keeping its head absolutely still. Among the larger birds of prey, the short-eared owl patrols the fells in broad daylight in search of field voles, its favourite victim. Often looking quite pale, it has long wings and a slow swaying flight. The occasional buzzard or even a hen harrier are seen on the fells from time to time, so be prepared for such an event.

Two outstanding species of the high scars and crags (*walks 8 and 20*) are the peregrine and the raven. Peregrines have had a major comeback in the last thirty years and numbers have risen appreciably, but now they are in danger of being taken for falconry in Europe and the Middle East at black market prices. The bird is the greatest of hunters, and to watch its power dive or 'stoop' is a thrilling experience. The raven, too, is an impressive bird, being nearly half as big again as a crow. It can be distinguished by its habit of soaring, its powerful wing beats, long primary feathers and acrobatic flight.

In all parts of the dale one is likely to see the black-headed gull, which breeds in large numbers near various small reservoirs and tarns. When seen close up, it is unmistakably a gull, but seen at a distance in poor light, its effortless gliding flight can deceive the unwary birdwatcher into thinking that it is a bird of prey. Another common bird throughout the dale is the lapwing – a handsome bird with a distinctive crest. Its acrobatic display flights on broad black and white wings and its 'pee wit' calls provide a happy distraction for the walker.

Mammals on the fells include voles, stoats and hares. Few live on exposed mountain tops, but field voles live on the upland grass where they find shelter in burrows amid the tussocks of bilberry and heather. Stoats thrive on the voles and even meadow pipits, while foxes look out for carrion such as a dead hare or sheep. The brown hare with its long, black-tipped ears is larger than the rabbit and, like the rabbit, frequents the lower slopes (*walk 16*). The mountain hare doesn't live in the Dales area.

The small heath is a common butterfly of moorland areas and competes with the small tortoiseshell as the butterfly breeding at the highest altitude. The hardy green-veined white is another contender and is the most common white on high ground. The brightly-coloured small copper may be seen both on the moors and in the valley.

Woodland There are a few small patches of broad-leaved woodland: Freeholders Wood at Aysgarth Falls, the woods at Mill Gill near Askrigg, the wooded banks of the River Cover near Middleham and the wooded scars near West Burton. In this habitat there is a much greater variety of birds. The spotted flycatcher is a summer visitor and, although unremarkable to look at, is outstanding in its behaviour and well worth watching. About the size of a sparrow, it will perch upright on a branch and, exercising its long wings, dive for flies and regain the same perch time after time.

Its relative the pied flycatcher is more handsome – a little shorter and rarer, but a delight to see. Of the warblers, the willow warbler, blackcap and wood warbler can be distinguished by their song, but if you catch sight of them the wood warbler is more yellow-brown than the willow warbler, and it is the male blackcap that has the black

Spotted flycatcher.

cap, the female's cap being reddish-brown. A colourful summer visitor is the redstart, which likes open woodland or an over-grown hedge dotted with trees. Both the male and female have the orange-red tail, but only the male has a black face and grey upper parts.

The mouse-like treecreeper and sleek nuthatch may be seen at any time of year, though perhaps more easily when the leaves are off the trees. The tits tend to stay in the same area all year, and of course are residents in gardens and hedges too. The long-tailed tit is the most sedentary of all British birds and does not move more than a mile from its nest. The great spotted woodpecker likes a few old dead trees to inspect for grubs and insects, while the larger green woodpecker hunts on the ground for ants, making use of its long sticky tongue. The tawny owl is a special-ised nocturnal hunter, and you are most likely to hear its call when it becomes active at dusk. During the day you might see it perched in a tree close to the trunk.

Roe deer have become numerous in Wensleydale. You might even see these delightful amimals grazing in the fields with sheep or cattle, but the woods of the scars and the riverside provide cover for these small deer (*walks 10 and 16*). Also, in the more wooded parts of the dale, badgers have their territories. Active mainly at night, these beautiful animals are rarely seen, though the striped face is unmistakable when caught in a headlamp's glare

Rivers and Becks   The dipper likes the waterfalls of the dale, and is as much at home on a small rushing beck as on the wider river (*walk 2*). Similarly, the grey wagtail can be found along small becks and streams where the water is fast-flowing. Sandpiper and red-shank are commonly seen along the Ure in the summer months (*walks 5 and 7*) as they seek out crayfish, snails and insect larvae, while sand martins wing overhead, helping to reduce the flying insect population. The plant-eating mallard, moorhen and coot are resident along the river, and Canada geese gather in appreciable flocks (*walks 5 and 7*). Although the Canada goose is entirely vegetarian, the other three supplement their diet with insects and snails, and the less favourite coot will take eggs and young birds. The fish population provides a good food supply for the kingfisher and heron, as well as the great crested grebe (*walk 15*). It is wonderful to see the kingfisher: in flight a flash of blue, then turning to orange as it comes to rest and faces you on an overhanging branch. The handsome oystercatcher is now a common sight near the river with its striking black and white coat, long orange bill and sedate walk.

The goosander breeds on the Ure in hollow trees or holes in the riverbank. This diving duck is a sawbill – from the toothlike serrations along the sides of the long, narrow bill – and its food is fish. The

elegant male appears to be black and white, but a shaft of sunlight will reveal that his head is a gleaming dark green, like shot silk. The less spectacular female has a grey and white body and a reddish-brown head with a shaggy nape.

The native crayfish is worth a mention as it inhabits much of the river and many of the smaller tributaries too. The Yoredale Natural History Society are making a survey of this surprisingly large crustacean. It grows up to seven inches (18cm) long, and seems to like cold, oxygen-rich water in which there is dissolved lime. The crayfish used to be caught locally and cooked as a delicacy, rather like lobster.

The otter has the distinction of being a rarity as well as a favourite among wildlife enthusiasts. The problem is, it needs long stretches of undisturbed riverside and even then is seldom seen. Wensleydale is fortunate in having one site where this lovely animal has made its home. The water vole is a plump, round-faced animal with small ears and soft shaggy fur. Its body measures eight inches (20cm) long and the tail almost another five inches (12cm). Look out for it in a slow-moving river or stream with low banks and good vegetation cover. You may see one plop into the water as it swims away.

Along the river, in the lower dale, the orange-tip butterfly is common in May, and the peacock has become more numerous in recent years. The migrant red admiral and painted lady, both superb fliers, may be found across the dale at all altitudes.

Semerwater (walk 15)   In spite of activities of boating, fishing and windsurfing, there is usually something for the birdwatcher here. Mallard, tufted duck and coot are here all year, but it is nice to be fairly sure of a sighting of great crested grebe. This large, slender-necked bird is an expert diver and is rarely seen out of the

Goosander.

Great crested grebe.

water. In the breeding season it has a black crest and chestnut frills on each side of its head, and has a head-shaking courtship display. More rarely seen in the dale is the little grebe; much smaller with a short bill and neck, it flies more readily and performs a love duet in its courtship.

In winter, small flocks of whooper swans from Iceland visit Semerwater. This swan is distinguished by its black and yellow bill, and stiff, upright neck. Groups may graze on pasture next to the lake. Wigeon and goldeneye are other winter visitors. The wigeon is a short-necked dabbling duck and the male has a chestnut and cream head. The goldeneye is a black and white sea duck with a white spot on each cheek, and likes to dive and swim underwater.

Farmland The brightly-coloured yellowhammer is a resident farmland bird (*walk 1*), though never common. Fields bordered by hedges containing odd tall trees and a few brambles provide the right sort of habitat. The yellow head and chestnut rump are distinguishing features. The redstart may be thought of as a woodland bird, but frequents hedgerows in similar surroundings to the yellowhammer. In addition to the fells, farmland is also a common breeding place for the lapwing. Starlings and pied wagtails are also well adapted. Magpies and crows like tall trees in which to nest, and in the spring both will take eggs and young birds. For most of the year jackdaws and rooks live in mixed flocks and are typical farmland birds. Pheasants are very common along the dale, including melanistic and albino varieties, and both the grey partridge and the less common red-legged partridge occur.

The ideal habitat of the little owl is open fields and hedgerows and, active during the day, this small bird of prey is often seen perching in a prominent place. The wood pigeon is the biggest of the pigeons, with its white neck and wing patches, and is an unusually tame bird. In the autumn, flocks of fieldfares and redwings raid the berries on hawthorns, rowan and holly trees and may be accompanied by song and mistle thrushes. Occasionally a group of colourful waxwings arrive from Scandinavia.

The fox is a very adaptable and resourceful animal and can live on the fells, in the woods, on farmland or close to human habitation, and varies its diet accordingly. It tends to rest during the day and forage at night, hunting rabbits, voles, beetles or fruit, depending on what is available.

Farms and Villages Swifts find the gaps in the Yorkshire flagstone roofs of old barns and farms just big enough for them to squeeze through so they can build their nests in the roof. Since swifts never land on the ground, nests tend to be a bit scrappy and short of building material. The swallow may use a similar entrance, or the door or window of an outbuilding. It collects pellets of wet mud to cement its nest to a corner or beam. House martins often make use of the eaves on the outside. They are experts at nest-building and take 2,500 beakfuls of mud for a complete nest, which is then lined with feathers and grass.

The colourful goldfinch is a bird you will often find near a village. Thistle seeds are its favourite food, and before these are ripe it will feed on dandelion and grounsel. Another seed-eater is the attractive greenfinch, now common on bird tables. Other common birds around buildings and gardens include the friendly robin, the cheerful wren, house sparrow, dunnock, collared dove, blue tit, great tit and coal tit. With all these small birds around it isn't surprising that the sparrowhawk may not be far away. This bird is a superior hunter, swift, silent and deadly. It will even invade the bird table to take its prey.

One of our most familiar mammals is the grey squirrel, which seems to live happily in hedgerow trees, gardens and parkland without large areas of woodland, unlike the red squirrel which requires forests, especially of pine and larch. The grey squirrel is common in the dale and most people find its behaviour attractive, even though they too will mercilessly raid the bird table.

FLORA

What an exciting place Wensleydale is for wild flowers! The banks of the Cover near Middleham, the woods of Mill Gill and Aysgarth, the watery edges of the River Bain near Semerwater, the limestone scars and the riverside meadows are all havens for the most amazing collection of flowering plants. On a summer's day in a flowery meadow you might well believe you are in paradise. And if you see Wensleydale in the autumn there is a second brilliant flush of colour as the berries of wild arum, woody nightshade, rosehips, haws, sloes and black bryony decorate the hedgerows.

These plants have had a considerable amount of attention paid to them over the years by several eminent botanists who have lived in the dale. The famous physician and botanist Dr John Fothergill lived at Carr End Farm, Semerwater, and his nephew John Fothergill of Askrigg published the first plant list in 1823, when he noted 121 species. Dr Arnold Lees lived near Hawes for a time and added his records, published in the *Naturalist* in 1885. The first comprehensive flora for Wensleydale was written by Professor John Percival of Carperby, who recorded 583 species in 1888. A hundred years later, with the help of the local WEA and the Yoredale Natural History Society, Deborah Millward produced *A Flora of Wensleydale* which records 800 species.

Soils Plant communities reflect the wide variety of soils in the dale, so it is worth a brief look at the reasons for the rapidly-changing soil types. Because the soils of Wensleydale were removed during the Ice Age and new soils only began to form after the ice melted some 15,000 years ago, they are considered young and are labelled immature. Such soils closely reflect the underlying geology which, as we have seen, varies abruptly over short distances with so many bands of limestone, sandstone and shale, a plastering of glacial till and river deposits of the flood plain.

There are two other factors which have a marked effect on the soil. The first of these is 'slope'. Flat areas on the fell tops and valley floors are poorly drained and peat can form here, whereas the steeper slopes have good drainage and attract a richer flora. The lower parts of slopes have the best soils since, due to gravity, they are thicker and richer in minerals which have collected from higher up. The other factor is rainfall. High up on the fells and at the head of the dale, rainfall is heavy, being over 70 inches (1,800mm) per year, and soluble minerals are washed down through the soil, a process known as leaching. Lower down the dale the annual total is less than half this – Leyburn has only 30 inches (750mm). Basic (calcareous) soils become established only where rainfall is lighter and where calcium minerals have less chance of being washed down.

Some Key Plants Certain plants have such special requirements that their distribution can be shown to coincide with changes in rainfall, amount of sunshine or height above sea level, as well as types of soil. For example, rainfall totals affect the carline thistle, which likes to grow in the driest parts of the dale, so is not found higher up than Askrigg. The fact that Wensleydale lies in an east-west direction means that one side of the valley faces the sun and the other is north-facing and more shady. This affects the distribution of certain plants like the small fern, green spleenwort, which prefers the shady, north-facing side. Horseshoe vetch and green-winged orchid prefer the sunny, south-facing slopes (*walk 6*), and Wensleydale forms the northern limit of the European distribution of these two plants. As for altitude, cloudberry (*walk 8*) grows only above 1,650 feet (500m), whereas bistort, for example, mainly below 800 feet (250m).

The toxic soils around leadmine tip heaps attract the little starry flowers of spring sandwort and, near the road by the Woodhall mines, sea thrift and scurvygrass, together with the sandwort, form a rare carpet of pink and white in the early summer.

Spring sandwort.

A Transect from the Fell Top to the River Ure

Dr Arnold Lees claimed that, among the Yorkshire dales, Wensleydale:

'. . . ranks second only to Teesdale in the richness and variety of its plantlife. This is . . . by reason of the successive alternations of shales, flagrock, limestones and grits which its slopes present, from the Yore bed at 500 feet altitude to the fell ridges at over 2,000 feet.'

The area of limestone exposed is relatively small and is often covered by glacial debris, but in the upper dale the scars of Hardraw and Simonstone limestones produce strips of bright green pasture along the sides of the valley, each having typical limestone plants. Below Bainbridge the long horizontal bands of ash and beech woods mark the same limestones scars.

To get an idea of the rapid changes in species from one place to another, let's start high up on the fells and look at the sorts of wild flowers that grow on the tops, then on the limestone scars and intervening slopes down to the glacial till and valley floor below:

The high fells:

On Penhill and Dodd Fell (*walks 8 and 19*), cottongrass, heather, bilberry and cloudberry all grow well on the acid peaty soil. Cloudberry is one of the brambles and creeps along the ground, but is easy to spot because of its bright green leaves and striking white flowers. Close inspection of boggy areas among the sphagnum may reveal cranberry, a little beauty with pink, dart-shaped flowers, the petals curled back like a small cyclamen.

High limestone scars:

The two high limestones are the Main limestone, as on Ellerkin Scar, and the Underset limestone, seen on Ivy Scar and the top of Addlebrough. The soils on these strata are thin, become leached by heavy rain and tend to be on the acid side of neutral. It is here that the mountain pansy is most at home. The yellow form is the most common, but purple forms and half yellow, half purple types can be found. In July hundreds of them are in flower, dotted about Ox Close above Carperby (*walk 12*). Two more typical plants are the variable coloured milkwort and the rare and attractive mountain everlasting flower, which grows only on these two limestones. On the bare rock of the scar, out of reach of the sheep, scurvygrass, the tiny rue-leaved saxifrage, small scabious, biting stonecrop and green spleenwort all find a footing.

High scree slopes:
Below the high scars, the scree slope tends to have a rather thin, well-drained, alkaline soil, and this is the habitat of mossy saxifrage. This plant is more common on the south side of the dale on the shady, north-facing slopes. Where growing near lead spoil it varies in colour with pink or cream forms, and is common by the Roman road above Burtersett (*walks 15 and 17*).

Lower slopes:
Here the soil is thicker, fairly well drained and slightly acid. Heath bedstraw and thyme-leaved milkwort are usually found together, and harebell grows along with tormentil.

The Hardraw limestone:
This is a very persistent band at an altitude of about 800 feet (250m) and carries good sheep pastures on thin alkaline soils. The lawnmower efficiency of grazing sheep, however, narrows the range of species to hardy plants such as white clover, daisy, pignut, creeping buttercup and germander speedwell. Where there are bare limestone cliffs on the Hardraw limestone, these support herb robert, hairy rockcress, limestone bedstraw and the ferns, western polypody and brittle bladder fern. In fact, the scars have the most undisturbed vegetation in the dale, being of no use to man and out of the reach of sheep.

Lower scree slopes:
On scree slopes below the Hardraw limestone the soils are rich and basic, supporting a wide variety of flowering plants. Many of these slopes below the scars are still wooded, such as on Thornton and Worton (*walk 16*) scars on the south side of the dale, and Nappa and Woodhall scars across on the north side. Flowers

Some leaf shapes (clockwise from top left): sycamore, ash, beech, sessile oak, pedunculate oak and hazel.

include herb bennet, cowslip, early purple orchid, wild marjoram and in the wooded areas, primroses, common violet, bluebell, St John's wort, water avens and wild garlic.
Glacial till:
Below the Hardraw limestone on both sides of the valley floor there are rolling hills of glacial material in the form of drumlins and moraines (*walk 7*). Although of glacial origin, they are calcareous and often provide a rich and fascinating collection of flowers. Deborah Millward recorded an amazing list of nearly forty plants, including four or five orchids, on the north side of a drumlin in the middle of a hay field. The steep slopes are well drained and often too steep to mow, and make exciting territory for the botanist.

A Woodland Habitat   There is a wonderful array of flowers to be seen in Freeholders Wood (*walk 10*) at Aysgarth Falls. Here is, for Wensleydale, a rare patch of broad-leaved woodland with a mixture of hazel, ash and oak, and other species such as bird cherry, hawthorn and holly. The woods at Aysgarth Falls are on glacial moraine and the soil is calcareous. The two primulas, cowslip and primrose, both grow here and occasionally the hybrid form false oxlip may be seen, like a multi-headed primrose. Bluebell, dog's mercury, wild garlic, arum lily and wood anemone are all fairly common flowers. There are six speedwells (species of *Veronica*), which include the pale blue wood speedwell with its lime-green leaves, the deep blue germander speedwell and *V beccabunga* or brooklime, which is frequent on the muddy paths through the wood. Early purple orchid grows here, as does the strange green flower of herb paris, the presence of which is a sure sign of an ancient wood. Herb bennet and water avens, together with their own hybrid, are present, and goldilocks, wood cranesbill, wood sanicle

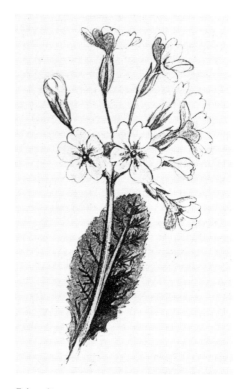

False oxlip.

and yellow pimpernel are other woodland species. Honeysuckle brings fragrance to the wood, guelder rose adds further colour, and both have bright red berries in the autumn.

The beech woods of Mill Gill (*walk 14*) near Askrigg and the banks of the Cover upstream from Cover Bridge near Middleham are also worth visiting to see woodland trees and flowers. Here are some of the tall, grey-barked beeches which are becoming a rarity in the dale. The silky leaves and long pointed buds make it easily recognisable and the spiny nuts or 'mast' are edible.

Toadstools are most common among deciduous trees, especially in the autumn. The smell of the stinkhorn reaches you long before you find the culprit. Shaggy ink

25

cap, which dissolves into black ink, and the poisonous, spotted, red fly agaric are two well-known fungi. Boletes are woodland types which are often large and colourful and have a spongy texture under the cap instead of gills. Puffballs are more common in fields and pastures, like the edible mushroom.

Watery habitats Around Semerwater (*walk 15*) there is a wealth of water plants. Just above the lake is a small nature reserve managed by the Yorkshire Wildlife Trust, a marshy area where globeflower, early purple and common spotted orchid are to be found. Along the lake shore grow the handsome bogbean, marsh ragwort, yellow water lily and marsh cinquefoil. Just below Semerwater Bridge the River Bain starts off by meandering through banks of thatching reeds, tall grasses and rushes,

Bogbean.

meadowsweet, water ragwort, watermint, devilsbit scabious and great burnet, while the large oval leaves and bright flowers of the yellow water lily grace the slow-moving surface and amphibious bistort dislays its pink spikes above the water.

In the lower part of the dale, Pinkers Pond (*walk 3*), Fish Pond and the ponds below Jervaulx Abbey (*walk 1*) all attract water-loving plants. The bulrushes at Jervaulx are particularly impressive and make good shelter for water birds.

The rushing waters of the gills (*walk 14*) provide moisture for clumps of opposite-leaved golden saxifrage and bog stitchwort, with a profusion of mosses and liverworts. The limestone flushes are a special habitat for the lovely pink birdseye primrose and the insect-eating, purple-flowered butter-wort.

Wensleydale is a great haunt for the flower lover, and the best time of year to see them is from about the middle of May to the end of June when new flowers come out with every week that passes. There are so many species to look out for that it is only possible to learn a few at a time. So notice those that are similar to the ones you know – the 'look-alikes' which look the same but are somehow different. Keep a flower book handy, such as Franklyn Perring's *Guide to British Wild Flowers*, to help sort them out. Make a list with the date and location, and jot down simple descriptions of new or problem ones. It doesn't take long to get to know not just the names of the flowers, but some further rare snippets of information which add considerably to their interest and appreciation.

Climate The weather is mostly better down the valley, so if it is raining or cloudy in Hawes, try a walk round Jervaulx instead, where you may bask in the sun all day. The east-west trend of Wensleydale results in a great range of climatic conditions between high and low ground, and from one end of the dale to the other. By far the wettest part of the dale is the Moorcock end, which has 70 inches (1,800mm) of rain a year, two and a half times as much as Jervaulx, which has only about 27 inches (700mm). So there is much more chance of a dry day in the eastern part of the dale.

Some months – particularly February, April, May and June – have have less than average amounts of rainfall, whereas August to January tend to be wetter than average. The heaviest rain often comes with thunderstorms, which are most likely to occur in the warmer months of July and August. So the best time of year for walking is in the spring and early summer, when there is less likelihood of rain and the footpaths are relatively dry – which, incidentally, coincides with the best time for birds and flowers.

Winters are often long and cold, spring being drier and coming later than on the west of the Pennines. Summers tend to be short, though autumns can stay mild until November. The great variation in climate throughout the year and from one place to another ensures a great range of habitat for plants and wildlife.

WALK 1: JERVAULX ABBEY AND THORNTON STEWARD

Start: Jervaulx Abbey car park. Grid Ref: 169 856
Distance: 7½ miles (12km)
OS Maps: Pathfinder 630 (Middleham and Jervaulx Abbey) or Landranger 99
Walking Time: 4 hours

This is an easy, flat walk through lower Wensleydale. It starts with a stroll through the impressive ruins of Jervaulx Abbey, renowned for its interesting flora. The walk crosses the Ure at the ancient Kilgram Bridge, returns through Thornton Steward and visits the old church of St Oswald. Danby Hall, Ulshaw Bridge and Cover Bridge are all on the route, which finishes with a walk along the bank of the river.

Jervaulx Abbey is in the grounds of Jervaulx Old Hall, now a hotel. From the car park, cross the road and pass the hotel entrance to reach the abbey. Information is available about the ruins as well as a checklist of the flowers. It is well worth the time to wander round. Through the centuries, stone from the abbey has been used in local buildings. However, the remains are still impressive in extent and the finest part is the ruined dormitory with its many lancet windows. With a little imagination, something of the importance of the abbey can be gained when you think that at the height of its prosperity it owned half of Wensleydale.

There is a story of the first abbot who was travelling with twelve monks to Fors Abbey (the site is near Askrigg) when they lost their way in thick woods, but were guided by a vision of the Virgin Mary who said: 'Ye are late of Byland but now of Yorevale'. So the abbey came to be founded by the River Ure in 1156 and named Jervaulx, the French way of saying 'Yorevale'. The monks were Cistercians who lived very simply in silence and who worked the land, made cheese and bred horses. The cheese was formerly made from ewes' milk, but its manufacture has persisted through the years to the Wensleydale we know so well today. Similarly, the breeding of horses has

also continued and prospered, with the specialisation in racehorses during the last 200 years.

In 1536 came the dissolution of the monasteries, a disastrous occurrence for the local people. The abbeys were the lifeblood of the community, being centres for farming, craftsmanship, learning and trade. Because of this, Abbot Sedbergh was encouraged by the ordinary people to join the Pilgrimage of Grace, the revolt against the dissolution. He fled to Witton Fell as a refuge, but in retaliation Jervaulx was almost totally destroyed, and the abbot was taken to London and hanged at Tyburn.

It is an attractive place for many birds. The song thrush is common but in summer look out for the spotted flycatcher, a small grey-brown bird with pale streaked underparts. It can be recognised by its habits more than its shape or plumage: it will perch in an upright position and acrobatically dive to catch flies, returning to the same place, or will hover to take insects from leaves or bark. Spotted flycatchers build a small, neat nest among climbing plants against a wall and, when fledged in June, family groups are noisy and attract attention.

Jervaulx is notable for the variety of its wild flowers growing on the ruins. In her book *Wild Flowers of the Yorkshire Dales*,

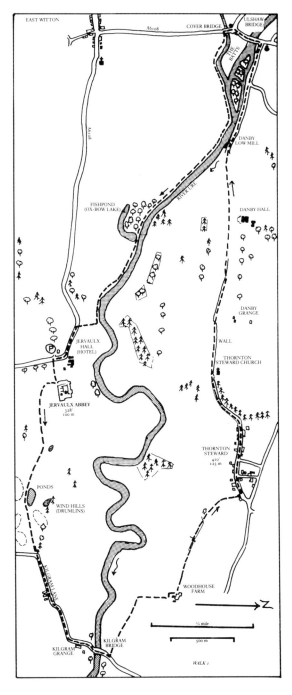

Sylvia Arnold puts them into three groups: relics from the gardens of the old monks, which include aubretia, lilac and snapdragon; examples of flowers introduced later, such as feverfew, ivy-leaved toadflax and yellow stonecrop; and natural wild flowers of the limestone, like shining cranesbill, viper's bugloss and musk mallow. Just a few of these species can be a riot of colour, and the old walls provide an ideal rock garden and romantic background for them. Feverfew has white daisy-like flowers with yellow centres and grows to twenty inches (50cm) – it was introduced as a herb of great medicinal value. Ivy-leaved toadflax which decorates the old walls has a purple flower like a miniature snapdragon. The lip of the flower is yellow and acts as a honey guide to pollinating

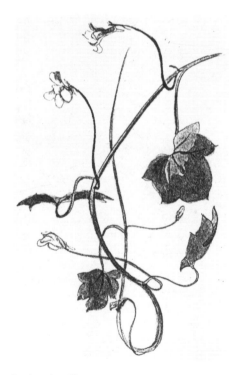

Ivy-leaved toadflax.

bees. It was introduced in about 1640 from the Mediterranean for garden rockeries. Yellow stonecrop, also known as wall pepper, grows in clusters of bright yellow flowers in the summer.

On leaving the ruins, go straight forward from the entrance to join a gravel track through Jervaulx Park to the left. There are groups of trees in this parkland setting, with pines, oaks and beeches and new plantings further on. The path goes between low hills and passes two ponds, the larger of which has bulrushes growing along its edge, and swans, moorhen and coot in residence. The rounded hillocks are drumlins formed during the Ice Age, when glacial material made up of a mixture of clay, sand and rocks was moulded into these shapes beneath the ice. The long axis of each hill runs parallel to the direction of ice flow, and groups of them form attractive miniature hill scenery.

Arrive at the road by the lodge cottage and turn left to pass Kilgram Grange Farm to reach the old Kilgram Bridge. Its six powerful stone arches have stood here at least since the 1540s when John Leland described it as 'a great old bridge of stone'; so it could easily be a hundred years older than this and thus one of the oldest road bridges in Yorkshire. The bridge is surrounded by tall trees which are a great show in the autumn. Looking upstream the river flows peacefully but the downstream view shows a rushing river, and from April the sandpiper takes up its territory along here. This small wader is olive brown above and white beneath with brown sides to its breast, and very difficult to see among the stones. It doesn't stay still for long, however, as it rocks its body backwards and forwards. Its flight is very distinctive, flicking and gliding over the water with curved wings. You may hear the piping 'tsee-wee-wee' long before you see the bird that makes it.

A stone embalming trough at Jervaulx Abbey.

Go over Kilgram Bridge and notice the raised, arched walkway built to keep feet out of the mud on the approach to the bridge. Turn left through two lots of double gates and across a field to a stile marked by a white post, through a meadow to a metal gate at the far top corner and turn right to reach Woodside Farm. Turn left at the farm across the fields, striking up to the right to the village of Thornton Steward. The yellowhammer does not seem so common as it used to be, but you may hear it as you cross the farmland. Its 'little-bit-of-bread-and-no-cheese' song is easy to recognise, ending with a long 'chwee', and the yellow plumage on head and underparts is striking. The yellowhammer is with us all year and feeds on seeds, berries, shoots and insects.

Thornton Steward is a quiet little village sited even off the minor roads. Its verges are enhanced with pinkish-purple wood cranesbill in May, and at the far end of the village is the manor house and farm. The route takes you past the farm and down the narrow road to St Oswald's Church. The church is particularly interesting to visit. It stands away from Thornton Steward, and because of this it is thought that it may have been surrounded by a village that was wiped out by the plague. The rounded arch over the door is Norman, but the small rectangular plan without aisles suggests it may have been of Anglo-Saxon foundation. Inside, the broad sepulchral arch is where an Easter liturgical drama took place in medieval times. There are the remains of ninth or tenth century crossheads in the church.

Go through the wooden gate and across a cart track in the up-dale direction. Pass through a metal gate, first keeping the wall on the right and crossing it to keep it on the left. The route is through the parkland scenery of the grounds of Danby Hall, where members of the Scrope family once lived. Go in front of the hall and on to Low Danby Mill to join a road. At the Catholic church at Ulshaw, built for the Scropes, turn left over Ulshaw Bridge and the River Ure, another fine, four-arched old bridge with a seat and sundial. The latter bears the date 1674. The width between the parapets is only twelve feet (3.6m), so the recesses are most useful for walkers. A little further on is the Cover Bridge Inn.

The innkeeper was traditionally the holder of the recipe for Wensleydale cheese, passed down by the monks of Jervaulx Abbey. Coverdale now has its own cheese with a tangy taste. From the pub go over the bridge, the last one over the Cover river. It has a single semi-circular arch and is probably eighteenth century. Turn left to start a delightful riverside stretch, first along part of the River Cover in its final stage before it joins the Ure, then along the bank of this now mature, meandering river. In spring the butterbur pushes up its flowery heads and bird cherry trees produce masses of white flower spikes. By early summer the butterbur is just as conspicuous by its bold, white seedheads, and as often as not the bird cherry is covered in the tent-like cobwebby cocoons of the bird cherry ermine moth. In the autumn, mushrooms grow well along here. A hedge has been newly planted along the field boundary which, as it grows, will benefit the wildlife of the area.

The confluence of the two rivers is almost hidden from view and comes after the Ure divides round three large wooded islands, known as the Batts. It is said that here the kelpie or waterhorse haunts the river, rising out of the mist to lure victims into the water. Across the Ure stands Low Danby Mill, which once made use of the river's water power by means of the the weir. To stroll along the riverside path in May is like walking through a flowery meadow, with the bright yellows, blues and reds of buttercup, speedwell, and red clover and other flowers.

This contrasts with grazed banks further on, where a flood sign shows 310 feet (95m) above sea level, and swallows and sand martins swoop and dive incessantly over the water as they hunt for flies. Swallows tend to nest in old farm buildings, but the sand martin makes a tunnel in a sandy part of the riverbank. You can distinguish the sand martin from the swallow by its brown breast band and its shallow forked tail, and it lacks the white rump of the house martin. Both swallows and sand martins often return to the same nest sites year after year. The banks of both sides of the river have raised levées which prevent flooding and which the path follows for the most part. On reaching the road, turn left to arrive at the abbey car park once more.

WALK 2: EAST WITTON AND THE RIVER COVER

Start: East Witton. Grid Ref: 143 860
Distance: 4½ miles (7km)
OS Maps: Pathfinder 630 or Landranger 99
Walking Time: 2½ hours

The attractive village of East Witton is only a mile or so (2km) from Middleham off the A6108. This beautiful walk starts here, and the highlight is the stretch along the wooded banks of the River Cover where in spring and early summer there is an abundance of wild flowers and woodland birds. It is a walk for the family and not to be hurried, passing over Hullo Bridge and returning through the fields. There is parking by the green in East Witton.

East Witton lies just within the Yorkshire Dales National Park at the foot of Witton Fell, the steep slopes of which provide the beginnings of the dale landscape. Although the village once had a market, the plague of 1563 was so bad that the market was moved to Ulshaw Bridge and as a result the importance of the village declined. The present houses in the village face each other across a wide green, planted with groups of flowering cherry and other trees. The village green was preserved when the houses were rebuilt in 1809 by the Earl of Aylesbury, who followed an early village plan of 1627. The old plan also had five cottages on the green, but these were omitted when rebuilding took place, improving the layout and leaving a particularly large green. East Witton has a shop-cum-post office, the Blue Lion pub and a large church. The new church was built at the same time as the rest of the village, using stone from the old church at Low Thorpe, where today there are just a few gravestones among the trees. The building of it commemorated George III's fifty years as king. At the end of the green is a water tap attached to a big glacial boulder. In 1859, the three ton rock was dragged from a nearby field to its present position by a team of sixteen horses, and emphasises the importance of a good water supply.

Go through the gate to the left of the Methodist chapel. A series of stiles brings you to the river. After negotiating one of the stiles you have to jump immediately across Cold Kelds Beck, a sort of human Beechers Brook. On reaching the river, turn downstream along its bank to the eighteenth century Cover Bridge. The River Cover, pronounced to rhyme with hover, is about to join the Ure, and both rivers are noted for good fishing. There was an inn here when Jervaulx Abbey was a thriving community, and fishermen and travellers have used it ever since.

Cross the single, semicircular arched bridge and turn left, past the Cover Bridge Inn to a stile which leads back to the river on its other bank. Alders grow by the water, and blackthorn, elder, wild roses and holly give way to larger ash, sycamore and elm. This is a delightful ribbon of riverside woodland, rich in wildlife. The alder trees have catkins in February and by March the white blossom of the blackthorn, which comes out before the leaves, brightens the riverbank. The ash trees are the last to come into leaf; they cast little shade and prefer calcarious soils. The leaves have ten or a dozen pointed leaflets, and the winged fruit are the well-known ash keys.

In summer, at the edge of the wood, red campion grows on the rich soil and sweet

33

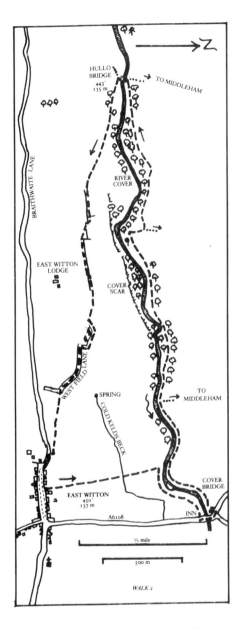

HULLO
BRIDGE
443'
135 m

TO MIDDLEHAM

RIVER
COVER

BRAITHWAITE LANE

EAST WITTON
LODGE

COVER
SCAR

WEST FIELD LANE

SPRING

COLD KELLS BECK

TO
MIDDLEHAM

COVER
BRIDGE

EAST WITTON
450'
137 m

A6108

INN

½ mile

500 m

WALK 2

'courtship and matrimony' reflects the two aromas: the strong perfume of the flowers representing courtship, while the less attractive scent of the crushed leaves is the reality of marriage!

In the spring, lesser celandine, wood anemone, bluebell and wild garlic enliven the woodland floor. The lesser celandine is one of our earliest wild flowers and its golden stars give a promise of spring, while the delicate, nodding wood anemone may carpet the ground, opening its lovely white petals when the sun shines. All these early flowers take advantage of the greater amount of light which comes through the leafless trees. By May, when the trees come into leaf, flowers like the celandine quickly die off. Notice the related wood avens and water avens. The yellow wood avens, *Geum urbanum*, also goes by the name of herb bennet after St Benedict, and this plant hybridises with the pink water avens, *Geum rivale*, to produce a drooping yellow flower which has characteristics of both.

This is a good place to see some woodland birds, and among a variety of summer visitors are the two flycatchers. The handsome, black and white male pied flycatcher is always on the move and you have to be quick to spot him. He is quite likely to have two mistresses to help build nests for, but will only feed the chicks of one of them. The pale, grey-brown spotted flycatcher is less distinguished, but its upright pose when perched and its acrobatic dive for a fly help to identify it. Listen, too, for the song of the willow warbler with its clear descending notes, and the blackcap which has a rich and varied warble, short and clearly phrased. The blackcap has been called the 'northern nightingale' because of its lovely song. Once you have heard it, look carefully and you may catch sight of it as it flies jerkily to a new perch. Its cap, glossy black in the male and brown in the female, make this summer visitor easy to identify.

woodruff by the path, its white flowers giving off a rich fragrance. By mid-summer another sweet-smelling flower, meadowsweet, is in bloom. Its Yorkshire name of

34

Wood avens (bottom) and water avens.

The footpath from East Witton to Middleham crosses our route and is marked by stepping stones in the river. It may hardly merit the name of river, but the running water of the Cover attracts the white-fronted dipper, which flies close to the surface or rests on a stone to bob up and down and flick its tail. It is a plump bird, and will plunge into the stream and swim under water or walk on the bottom in its search for a tasty morsel. The grey wagtail is another resident you are likely to see, and likes fast-flowing, pebbly streams and rivers. Its yellow underparts, whitish flanks and grey back make it a handsome bird. The female builds a nest of moss and grass, lined with hair, in a hole near the water. She may use the old nest hole of a dipper. They feed on flies and other insects.

Emerging from the woods, the path leads through a grassy area full of meadow flowers. A path goes off to Middleham from here. There is a great variety of plants and it is worth a pause to look at them. In the spring the primroses and cowslips have a beauty of their own. The Latin name of *Primula* means 'first rose' and refers to the early flowering. The cowslip is said to have sprung from the spot where St Peter dropped the keys to Heaven – so the flowers resemble a bunch of keys. Then

Pied flycatcher (male).

35

Dipper.

bugle and milkwort bring a change of colour – purple and blue – but milkwort can also be purple or white. In the summer come the deeper yellows of birdsfoot trefoil and rockrose, the white pignut and purple tops of knapweed. The pignut is a small, delicate member of the parsley family with fine feathery leaves. The knobbly tuber is edible, and children still enjoy finding them. Shakespeare knew this wild food, as Caliban in the *Tempest* declares: 'And I with

my long nails will dig thee pignuts'. Knapweed's other name of hardhead is most appropriate and describes the rounded flowerheads at the tip of each branching stem. It is a large plant, and the flower is purple and thistle-like in shape.

Climb up to the top of the steep, wooded bank. The path goes through fields above the wood, and after a while descends to Hullo Bridge. The proper name for the bridge is Ulla Bridge, but the map makers wrote Hullo for Ulla and so the name has stuck. Two footpaths and a bridleway cross the bridge, which has seen much use over the years. The bridge is in a good state of repair and makes a fine single stone span over the Cover, where here the river has cut down into limestone bedrock. It is a scenic spot and makes a good picnic place.

Having crossed Hullo Bridge, return along the right bank of the river the length of one field, then go up to a gate and up again across a meadow to cross a stile and small stream by a hawthorn hedge. After a metal gate, keep the hedge on the left until opposite the large farmhouse of East Witton Lodge, then follow the farm track with hedge on the right. Pass round the left side of a small plantation and into West Field Lane. Where the lane turns right, continue straight on through one or two finely-built stiles to join the road to East Witton village.

WALK 3: CALDBERGH AND COVERHAM FROM MIDDLEHAM

Start: Middleham. Grid Ref: 128 877
Distance: 7 miles (11km)
OS Maps: Outdoor Leisure 30 or Landranger 99
Walking Time: 4 hours

This is a lovely walk into the lower part of Coverdale and visits several historically interesting places, including the towering ruins of Middleham Castle, its predecessor on William's Hill, an Iron Age fort and the tranquil remains of Coverham Abbey.

Middleham is a small market town with two market places, and several hotels and restaurants. It grew up round the large Norman castle which dates from 1170. The town was awarded its market charter in 1389 and for a hundred years Middleham won great fame and fortune, becoming known as 'the Windsor of the North'. The powerful Neville family lived in the castle for several generations, including Richard Neville, Earl of Warwick, 'the Kingmaker'. The castle then went to King Edward IV's brother Richard, Duke of Gloucester, who married Richard Neville's daughter Anne and became Richard III of England. From the mid-seventeenth century the castle was in disuse and became a quarry for dressed stone for many of the fine houses which were built in the town. In Victorian times, various squatters and small businesses occupied the ruins, including a gang of sweeps, a cartwright, a blacksmith's shop, saw pits and a pack of hounds! Today the bulky ruins are still tall and impressive, cared for by English Heritage and well worth a visit. In June the walls are draped with the lovely purple flowers of fairy foxglove.

Start by going along the left side of the castle, over the second stile on the right and diagonally across to William's Hill. This is the site of the first timber castle of Middleham. Here, in an ancient deer park known as Sunskew, just 440 yards (400m) from

Middleham castle is a large earthwork. It is in a more elevated position with a motte (or mound) within a surrounding ditch and bank. A wooden fortification was built here soon after the conquest by Ribald, the nephew of William the Conquerer, and was in use until the stone castle was erected. It is said that for anyone who runs nine times round it, a door will open in the mound and immense treasure will be theirs.

From William's Hill, descend towards Middleham to a stile in a wall which takes you to Coverham Lane and the beginnings of Middleham Low Moor. Walk along the left edge of the unfenced road for 400 yards (365m) to a stile which leads diagonally across a field and down another to Hullo Bridge. What a pleasant spot this is, where the neat bridge spans the rocky bed of the River Cover. The map shows six tracks meet at the bridge and, as a result, many 'hullos' must have been said here over the years. You are now entering the Yorkshire Dales National Park, Middleham being just outside the park, and the next part of the walk is on National Trust land.

Follow the cart track up to Braithwaite Lane. Opposite you is an imposing view of Braithwaite Hall, a seventeenth century manor house set in beautiful gardens. It is possible to look round the building but only by prior arrangement, though it occasionally advertises tea and coffee or bed and breakfast. It is a private residence but

37

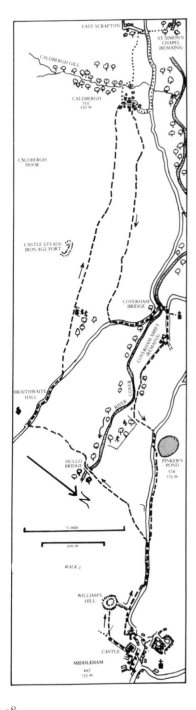

owned by the National Trust. The hall is on the site of an old grange of Jervaulx Abbey. Not far from Braithwaite Hall, between the hall and Coverham, is an old leadmine which was particularly rich in silver. The River Cover powered a large waterwheel to pump water from the mine, which closed in 1866.

Turn right along the road for about 440 yards (400m) to a stile on the left, where the path climbs up the hillside and then goes along the contour above a conifer wood. Just before reaching a barn, there is an interesting Iron Age hill fort 220 yards (200m) up on a shelf of the hillside to the left. It is known as Castle Steads Fort and was a fortified settlement of the Brigantes when they were having skirmishes with the Romans. Guerrilla warfare carried on until the Brigantes eventually lost power at the Battle of Stanwick. Another Brigantian fort stands less than a mile to the east at the back of Braithwaite Hall. As for the Romans, there are the remains of a Roman dwelling at Middleham and, on Witton Fell, Castaway Well used to be called Diana's Well. Diana the huntress was, no doubt, goddess over these hunting lands in those times. Much higher up on the hill top on the left is a cairn called Flamstone Pin. It is only 1,300 feet (400m) above sea level but tradition has it that you can see both the North Sea and the Irish Sea from here on a clear day. It is said that a Coverdale man built the cairn so that he could see it from his ship and be reminded of home.

A little further on, just before dropping down to the little village of Caldbergh, there is a fine view up the dale with Great Roova Crags high on the left, and straight ahead Little Whernside, with the end view of Great Whernside to the right of it. In 1488 Miles Coverdale was born in Caldbergh, and he was to become the first person to translate the complete Bible into English from the Latin and German

38

Braithwaite Hall.

versions. Some of his work, such as the psalms in the *Book of Common Prayer*, is still in use today. Caldbergh Hall is a fine building dated 1688 and now called Manor Farm, and there are several stone cottages which make up this quiet hamlet.

Caldbergh Gill is just beyond the village and a path (difficult to follow) goes on across the gill to East Scrafton, Caldbergh's twin community on the south side of the river. Over the road from East Scrafton, a footpath leads down near the river to the remains of St Simon's Chapel, and this can make an interesting detour, returning along the road to Caldbergh. The chapel was built in 1328 for the use of local people in winter, and a hermit lived there and acted as caretaker. He was known as the 'king's hermit' after Richard III, a patron of Coverham Abbey. It was a simple

structure, falling into disuse after the dissolution of Coverham Abbey in 1536 and today only a low rectangular wall remains. Next to it is a limekiln and, just beyond, a new wooden footbridge over the Cover, a good place for a picnic.

From Caldbergh, take the lane from the village which leads through a farmyard in the down-valley direction. It crosses a small wooded gill, along a field, then climbs up to the top corner of the next field to continue along a level terrace with extensive views of Coverdale below. Across from here on the other side of the valley you can see the racing stables of Brecongill, Ashgill, Tupgill, Ferngill and Thorngill. Coverham Abbey was the first to breed horses, and these large establishments reflect more recent successes of a very old tradition. The large house at Brecongill was where

Coverham Bridge.

John Mangles trained seven winners of the St Ledger in the early nineteenth century, and where John Osborne later lived and trained horses, which he entered regularly in the Derby. Today hundreds of fine racehorses are bred in these stables and exercised on nearby Middleham Low Moor.

Continue along to the road and turn left down to the beautiful Coverham Bridge, which in a steep, single arch takes you across the waters of the Cover. This tranquil spot was busier in the past. Five or six hundred years ago, when the mill, the abbey and the church were all in use, there was a thriving community here. An important packhorse track came through here from Bolton Priory and Kettlewell in Wharfedale and over Park Rash.

After crossing the bridge, turn right. Immediately on the left are the largely rebuilt abbey high mill and miller's house.

Go through the gate on the left to visit the church, which is now redundant, though it may still be visited. From this corner of the churchyard the church could neither be seen nor, with the constant sound of the water mill, could the bell be heard. It was founded about 1250 and was restored in the nineteenth century. One problem recorded in 1428 was that the church porch too often became littered with longbows, where people tripped over them.

Continue along the lane through the gatehouse arch to the ruins of Coverham Abbey, most of which lie in private grounds, though much can be seen from the path. The abbey was founded about 1202, having moved from Swainby near Thirsk. The monks were of the Premonstratensian Order, wore white robes and held services for Dalespeople. Two arches still stand in a garden, part of the nave of the church, some windows and several stone inscriptions survive, having been incorporated in the present seventeenth century farmhouse, including the amazing nine-light window which makes it look quite sumptuous. The fact is that when the abbey was dissolved in 1536 (it was among the first to be supressed) the local people lost the hub of their community. They depended on the abbey to trade their meat and wool. They lost employment there, where local men were taken on to work in the kitchens, brewery and bakehouse and women to do washing, and they lost a resting place for travellers. The dissolution was a disaster for the people of the dale.

Take the right hand path signed Pinkers Pond between some outbuildings, and a little further on pass a humble barn built on handsome, round stone pillars, probably originating from the abbey, then up to the left to the road. Pinkers Pond is a shallow spring-fed stretch of water where coot and mallard breed, with redshank, lapwing, curlew and meadow pipit nesting on the surrounding pasture, while swallows and swifts glide overhead. It can be a delightful scene in the spring, and many people stop here for a picnic or just to get off the road and enjoy the view. However, the pond has recently taken to drying up in warm summers to become a desolate area of dry mud.

From Pinkers Pond, walk along on the right of the road (note the Turner Trail seat by the wall corner) for nearly half a mile (1km) and go through the stile on the right by a sheep fold, turning left down two fields to arrive back in Middleham.

WALK 4: COVERDALE FROM CARLTON

Start: Carlton. Grid Ref: 068 847
Distance: 7½ miles (12km)
OS Maps: Outdoor Leisure 30 or Landranger 98 and 99
Walking Time: 4 hours

This is a lovely walk with lots of variety and many discoveries to be made in the peaceful setting of Coverdale, starting at the village of Carlton and visiting West Scrafton, Swineside and Horsehouse. The return is along the edge of the moor from Fleensop

Coverdale is the biggest of the dales which run into Wensleydale and has the air of being self-contained, with good farmland, several small villages, its own abbey, a colliery, flagstone quarries and leadmines. The tell-tale place names– Carlton, Scrafton, Caldbergh and Coverham – indicate the Angles settled here. Along the dale once ran the main highway from London to Richmond – as shown on Ogilby's map of 1675 – and from Skipton to Middleham it passed through Linton and Kettlewell, then steeply up over Park Rash and the high moors to enter Coverdale, keeping to the north side of the river through Horsehouse and Carlton. Stagecoaches and packhorse trains came this way, staying overnight in Coverdale villages. But today the main roads bypass the dale and leave it quiet and unspoilt. Its fine rural landscape was chosen for the Herriot television series *All Creatures Great and Small.*

Carlton is recorded in the *Domesday Book*, and this part of the dale was for centuries part of a royal hunting forest of the lords of Middleham. The hunters' stone by the roadside marks the top of the valley, Coverhead farm was originally called Hunter's Hall and the courts of the forest were held in Carlton. It is believed an ancient parliament was held on the large mound in the centre of the village. Today it is a sleepy place. Strung out along the road, it has the Foresters Arms, and some fine old stone cottages and houses, and few tourists.

Begin from the lower end of the village by turning right along Quaker Lane in the direction of the River Cover and West Scrafton. A walled path takes you to a field with a view across to Flamstone Pin, Roova Crags and lynchets in the fields on the opposite side of the valley. The lynchets form terraces one above the other, remnants of the Anglian and medieval style of strip farming. The path meets Goodman's Gill and follows it down to its meeting with the River Cover and Caygill footbridge. Climb up to the beginning of the limestone ravine in Caygill, then bear right to follow the signs up the lynchets to the village of West Scrafton. This peaceful and attractive village, once the home of colliers and quarrymen, now lies on a very quiet byroad, although it is the meeting place of half a dozen footpaths which lead to other small hamlets and up onto West Scrafton Moor.

Take the Carlton road out of the village, then almost immediately branch left on the little road to Swineside. Walk up this ridge for lovely views of Coverdale to the right and, over to the left, Roova Crags and Great Haw. Look out for goldfinches along here. They are often seen in groups, or 'charms' as they are called. You may see them feeding on thistles or other seed heads in the late summer and autumn. The goldfinch is a dainty bird, with its forked

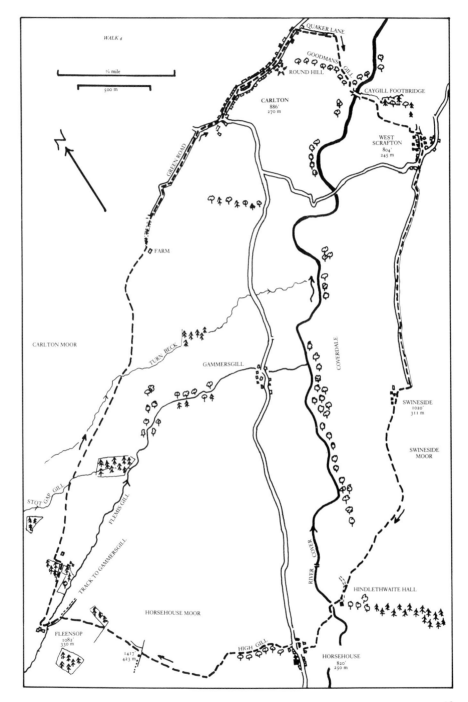

WALK 4

½ mile

500 m

QUAKER LANE

GOODMANS GILL

ROUND HILL

CAYGILL FOOTBRIDGE

CARLTON
886'
270 m

WEST
SCRAFTON
804'
245 m

GREEN ROAD

FARM

CARLTON MOOR

TURN BECK

COVERDALE

GAMMERSGILL

SWINESIDE
1020'
311 m

SWINESIDE
MOOR

STOT GAP GILL

FLEENSOP

FLEMIS GILL

TRACK TO GAMMERSGILL

RIVER COVER

HINDLETHWAITE HALL

HORSEHOUSE MOOR

FLEENSOP
1082'
330 m

1417'
423 m

HIGH GILL

HORSEHOUSE
820'
250 m

43

tail, a red face and the rest of the head black and white. In flight it shows the yellow wing-bar and white rump. Apart from the thistles, summer flowers along here include the bright pink of greater willowherb, the yellow-flowered meadow vetchling and purple betony. The leaves of the last plant were once favoured for a bitter herb tea.

Just before Swineside the view ahead reveals Dead Man's Hill and the flat-topped Little Whernside, with the end of Great Whernside to the right. An old pack-horse track goes from Horsehouse and Arkleside over Dead Man's Hill to Middlesmoor in Nidderdale, and is known to have been followed by packhorse trains and Scottish drovers. There are stories about lone Scottish pedlars whose route was over to Nidderdale and who mysteriously vanished, while certain wives in Nidderdale were wearing Paisley shawls. In 1728, three murdered, headless bodies were dug up at Lodge End, the first farm on the other side of Dead Man's Hill.

Turn right at the cattle grid and through the hamlet of Swineside. The Coverdale Country Hotel has taken up its retreat here, and the path bears left in front of the cottages and through the stile and fields to Horsehouse. The path keeps along the contour, then descends to a ladder stile and joins the track to Hindlethwaite Hall, an ancient manor house. Just before the farm, turn down to the right to find a footbridge over the river below an old barn, then through two more fields up to Horsehouse.

The name of the village may have come from the amount of packhorse traffic that used to pass this way *en route* from London to Richmond, and where horses were rested on the journey. The Thwaite Arms has the date 1808 on it. There is a National Park information board, a post office, church and tea garden, but don't miss the rare and old weeping beech tree in the churchyard.

Horsehouse.

To the left, beyond the Thwaite Arms, take the no-through-road past the former school house, which leads up High Gill and onto the rough grassland of Horsehouse Moor. After passing through the gate, follow the wall round to the right and more or less straight up the fellside to a gate on the crest of the moor. This is the habitat for moorland birds, and the first to be seen will be the meadow pipit. Another 'little brown bird', but the meadow pipit is worthy of closer scrutiny. Really an olive brown with white outer tail feathers, the 'mipit' has a varied song, notes which speed up as it rises in flight from the ground, turning to a whistling call as it descends with fluttering wings and tail up. Redshank and curlew, with their quality voices, breed here. There is nothing quite like the stirring call of the curlew in spring, its liquid notes, slow at first but accelerating to end in a bubbling trill. In its display flight the curlew rises sharply from the ground, hangs poised in mid-air and glides down on bowed wings.

From the top of the moor, bear right along the wall to the corner of a small wood. From here veer left, roughly in the direction of the electricity poles, to a gate onto the track to Fleensop farm. Turn left along the track, then curve round to the right at

Curlew.

Fleensop beneath large ash and sycamores to continue on the other side of the beck, called Fleemis Gill, towards Carlton.

Fleensop has been a small hamlet since the seventeenth century. Farming, coal-mining and leadmining have all created a good living here. Fleensop Colliery was a particularly busy coalmining area high above the farm on Fleensop Moor. Today there is a single farm at Fleensop, planned and developed by W J Lister who was born here. Much rough grassland has been reclaimed for meadow and pasture, and fine stone walls have been built. The farm rears milking cows and has a large flock of sheep.

After passing through a small wood and two gates, pass on the upper side of a barn to another gate and a fingerpost. The route is not so easy to follow and some map reading may be needed. Join another cart track but note the position of a ladder stile ahead. Then go above a pine wood and along the ridge bearing left and parallel with a little stream bordered with alders. Go straight foward to cross the stream and a small field then, without dropping height, continue to a gate at the far top corner of a large pasture. Aim to the left of the farm surrounded by sycamores to join a farm track which leads into a walled road. A green lane comes in from the left – a bridleway from West Burton in Bishopdale – and a right turn brings you into Carlton.

Here is a chance now to view the whole length of the village. There are some grand old houses, mostly eighteenth century, one of which has a stone inscription placed by the poet himself above the door with the words: 'Henry Constantine of Carlton the Coverdale Bard, Feb 14th 1861'. Another house has an ancient pear tree trained up the wall, and another is almost hidden now by three clipped yew trees.

Methodism is strong in Coverdale, where the tradition of the love feast is still held each summer. These include testimonies of faith and the celebrations start at West Scrafton, continue in Horse-house and end at Carlton. The Methodist chapel in Carlton, dated 1873, is built of local stone but with a tiled roof. Harking back to the days when the dale was a great hunting forest is another old tradition, the two yearly walk of the Coverdale Foresters. Starting in Carlton, it ends with celebrations at nearby Melmerby.

45

WALK 5: WEST WITTON FROM MIDDLEHAM

Start: Middleham. Grid Ref: 127 877
Distance: 9½ miles (15km)
OS Maps: Outdoor Leisure 30 or Pathfinder 99
Walking Time: 5 hours

Here is a lovely walk starting at the village of Middleham, easy going and with some lovely open views of the dale. It takes you across the broad expanse of Middleham Moor, on to West Witton, with a beautiful riverside return along the banks of the Ure. Parking in Middleham.

Middleham has many attractions, not least its formidable castle ruins steeped in the history of the Nevilles and Richard III. It has two market places, each with its cross, an interesting church, many fine houses and other buildings, and several pubs, cafes and restaurants. The Black Swan faces the White Swan and its ham and eggs are unrivalled. In the upper market place next to the fountain, erected for Queen Victoria's jubilee in 1887, is a bull ring once used for bull baiting, and the 'swine cross' is believed to commemorate the grant in 1479 of a twice-yearly fair and market by Richard, Duke of Gloucester (later King Richard III). The much-eroded, carved beast could represent Richard's emblem of a white boar, but the stone of the carving is magnesian limestone and different from the gritstone cross. The old grammar school, built in 1869, stands opposite. The crosses in both the upper and lower market squares are mounted on well-worn stone steps, the meeting and resting place of countless people over the centuries. The cross was regarded as a symbol of honest dealing, and was the proper place for buying and selling.

The church is mainly fourteenth and fifteenth century, built in the glorious days of the Nevilles and is dedicated to St Alkelda and St Mary. St Alkelda was a devout Christian who, it is said, was strangled for her beliefs near Middleham

by two Danish women. This may have taken place in the late ninth century during the early days of Danish settlement, when Viking gods were all powerful. The only other church dedicated to St Alkelda is that at Giggleswick near Settle. Inside the church there is the tomb slab of the last abbot of Jervaulx, Adam Sedbergh, leader of the Pilgrimage of Grace, and the fourteenth century font with its tall, elaborately-carved cover. The Rev Charles Kingsley was the last canon of Middleham, and the canon's stalls are still to be seen. A stained glass window of 1934 commemorates King Richard III and shows him with Queen Anne and their son.

From the path that goes along the left side of the castle, take the first stile on the right across the fields to come out onto Coverham Lane, where the path over Middleham Moor begins. This stretch of green turf is Low Moor, where racehorses are exercised each morning for most of the year. In the summer months they train on High Moor further west. There is plenty of open space here and the turf has just the right firm, cushioned surface to give the horses a good workout on the exercise gallops.

The path ascends the high part of the ridge to the left of a standing stone and a trig point. From here, there are wonderful views of Coverdale and Buckden Pike at its head on one side, and Wensleydale on the

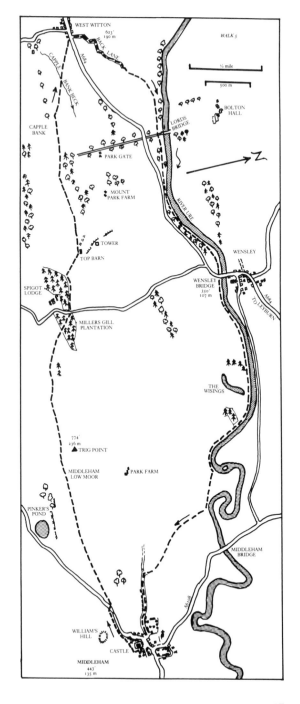

WEST WITTON
623'
190 m

WALK 5

¼ mile

500 m

BOLTON
HALL

CAPPLE
BANK

LORDS
BRIDGE

PARK GATE

N

MOUNT
PARK FARM

RIVER URE

TOWER

TOP BARN

WENSLEY

SPIGOT
LODGE

WENSLEY
BRIDGE
350'
107 m

TO LEYBURN

MILLERS GILL
PLANTATION

THE
WISINGS

774'
236 m
TRIG POINT

MIDDLEHAM
LOW MOOR

PARK FARM

PINKER'S
POND

MIDDLEHAM
BRIDGE

WILLIAM'S
HILL

CASTLE

MIDDLEHAM
443'
135 m

47

Middleham: the 'swine cross' and grammar school, and some racehorses.

other, with Penhill, Bolton Castle and a ruined tower towards which the walk continues. Follow the line of white stones which mark the edge of the practice race track. On the right is an area of gorse bushes and a small conifer plantation. Gorse is protected from grazing rabbits or even grazing horses because of its sharp spines, which are really modified leaves. The flower shows it to be a member of the pea family and the pods can be heard popping on a hot summer's day. Although a mass of brilliant yellow in the spring, there are usually some flowers out at all seasons of the year, and many a lover has sworn his eternal love 'as long as the gorse is in bloom'.

The route passes the corner of a wall to a stile, across a field and through Millers Gill Plantation, a fairly dense wood. The track crosses a small stream in the wood, and then goes up to the left and out to Hollins Lane. Cross the road and continue, with another plantation on the left, then diagonally across the next field to Top Barn. This is a very large and impressive barn with many arched stalls. The tower on the limestone knoll behind the barn is visible for much of the walk. It was built as a summer house by the third Duke of Bolton for Lavinia Fenton, who played Polly Peachum in Gay's *Beggars' Opera*. She was mistress of the duke, later becoming his second wife, and when she sang from the tower, her

48

voice, it is said, could be heard by the duke a mile away at Bolton Hall.

Don't go down the farm track but, without losing height, pass a lone ash tree to a gate in a wall. Keep the wall on the left and continue above the wood on the right. At the end of this pasture there is an interesting wet patch, where kingcups, marsh horsetail and soft and compact rush grow. Soft rush has a fairly thick, bright green, shiny stem, whereas compact rush has a thinner stem which is finely ridged.

From the next stile, continue straight forward to West Witton along a shelf of land below a scar, typical of Wensleydale scenery. This is Capple Bank, and higher up the slope and above Capplebank plantation is Middleham High Moor. From the next gate, drop down to a stile halfway along a fence and through fields dotted with flowers to West Witton. The village lies along the main road on a terrace below Penhill. It was the biggest village in the dale at the time of the Domesday record and contained many stone houses. The old Norman church, dedicated to St Bartholomew, was replaced by a new one in 1875, though the sixteenth century tower still remains. The village used to be a centre for the dyeing trade and is the birthplace of John James who wrote *The History of the Worsted Manufacture in England*, published in 1857. Witton Feast used to be a three day affair, though now it consists of the Cottage Show and the unique ceremony of 'The Burning of Owd Bartle', the Guy Fawkes of Witton.

Straight across the main road, the walk continues down Back Lane towards the river. There are some lovely flowers here in the spring and early summer. Among the blackthorn, wild roses and hawthorn there is the delicate cow parsley, often called keck in Yorkshire, vetch, which climbs the hedgerow using its tendrils, goosegrass, which children like to throw as it clings to

clothing, crosswort, another bedstraw with honey-scented yellow flowers, and white dead-nettle, with leaves rather like stinging nettle but with rings of white flowers which provide much valuable nectar for bumble bees. The mounds on the right of the lane are part of the lateral moraine of the Wensleydale glacier.

At the end of the lane, follow the wall on the left, drop to the lower level and veer right through the fields to Bay Bolton Avenue, with a view of Bolton Hall across the river. Walk down to Lord's Bridge to look at the river and the hall. The latter was built by the first Duke of Bolton and was partly rebuilt following a fire in 1902. Cross the avenue through a stile to the riverside footpath. There are one or two small plantations with woodland flowers and birds to look out for. Among the flowers are St John's-wort, which has been used to exorcise ghosts, bugle, used as a cure for all ailments, yellow pimpernel, as a pain killer, and woodsage, for brewing beer.

Wensley Bridge is an ancient and fascinating structure. Of beautifully dressed stone, it has four arches of differing shapes. The original bridge was built at the expense of John Alwine, a rector of Wensley who died in 1430. Richard Lord Scrope left £40 in his will in the year 1400 for its repair, and Leland in the 1540s wrote of this 'great bridge of stone'. So it could be fourteenth century. It had several repairs in 1586, 1637 and 1746, and was widened on the upstream side in 1818. You can see the two remaining of the three pointed arches from the older bridge on the downstream side.

Willow grows along the banks near the bridge, and flowers such as yellow rattle, red clover, plantain, sorrel and buttercup suggest an old hay meadow. In spring the next riverside part of the walk is excellent for birdwatching. Over the waters of the Ure the twittering swallows, swifts and sand martins fly continuously as they hunt

Shelduck.

for flies. The grey wagtail and the yellow wagtail are also expert at catching flies, though they like to watch from a perch such as an overhanging branch or a stone in the river. The yellow wagtail is a summer visitor, overwintering in West Africa. The male is an astonishingly brightly coloured bird, brilliant yellow below and greenish brown above. It is slim and graceful with a long tail, and you will see it dart about or flutter into the air after a fly.

Further along the riverbank a pond comes into view on the right, known as the Wisings, which attracts several water birds. Shelduck are present in the spring. This is the largest British duck, more like a goose

really, and is conspicuous by its black and white appearance and the chestnut band round its body. Coot with the white forehead, unmistakable grey heron, piping redshank, graceful mute swan and noisy oystercatcher also frequent this patch of water.

A line of ancient hawthorns and alders run parallel to the river, and soon the path leaves the bank at a gate to cross a large field to its far corner. Cross the cart track and take the path through the gate, straight up the field away from the river to the top left corner. The path leads onto Park Lane. Turn left here to reach the centre of Middleham.

WALK 6: LEYBURN SHAWL AND WENSLEY

Start: Leyburn. Grid Ref: 112 905
Distance: 5½ miles (9km)
OS Maps: Outdoor Leisure 30 or Landranger 99
Walking Time: 3 hours

This is an easy walk with panoramic views from Leyburn Shawl, a descent through the Keld Head leadmining area, a traverse of the grounds of Bolton Hall to the beautiful village of Wensley, and a visit to its outstanding church. The route continues through the fields and returns to Leyburn.

Situated at the top of a hill, Leyburn has grown into a busy and popular market town. It is of Anglian foundation and, although it was mentioned in the *Domesday Book* as 'Leborne', Leyburn did not really expand until the early nineteenth century, when many new houses were built. The church only dates from 1836. The coming of the railway in 1856 gave it another boost, and the town has been added to considerably in the twentieth century. It is the main centre for the dale: the auction mart takes sheep and cattle from miles around; it is an important shopping centre, has many hotels, cafes and restaurants; the large open air market still takes place in the square; children from the whole dale attend Wensleydale School, opened in 1959; the Richmondshire Council offices are in Thornborough Hall, surrounded by large gardens and woodland open to the public; and the Wensleydale Show is held here.

Leave the market place at the upper end, cross the road and follow the signs to the Shawl. The path soon comes out onto the edge of a high scar, with tremendous views across to Penhill, into Coverdale and up Wensleydale, with the flat-topped Addlebrough in the distance. This is Leyburn Shawl, a promenade laid out in 1841 with seats and shelters to attract the many fashionable visitors. It was here they were invited to tea galas with music and dancing, promoted by the Band of Hope and traders

who supported total abstinence. There was even a Leyburn Shawl annual festival, with concerts at the Bolton Arms. The coming of the railway brought many more tourists who liked to stroll along the Shawl and admire its famous view. The limestone terrace is a natural escarpment formed by the Main limestone. This grey rock, seventy-five feet (23m) thick, is extensively quarried near to Leyburn and large working quarries can be seen on the right of the footpath.

Many interesting flowers grow along the limestone scar, which has become well wooded in places. White deadnettle, St John's-wort, dovesfoot cranesbill and rockrose grow here in early summer. The delicate rockrose is rather a special flower. Its bright, golden-yellow petals attract insects for the pollen as the flower lacks scent or nectar, and if insects fail to pollinate, the petals close at night to ensure self-pollination. Dovesfoot cranesbill has small pink flowers and is related to herb robert. The name of dovesfoot refers to the rounded shape and softness of the leaf, which can turn red in the autumn. A mixture of trees include a few pines and larches but mainly the deciduous beech, ash and sycamore, with a scatter of smaller shrubs, hawthorn, blackthorn and elder. In spring the creamy clusters of scented elderflowers are a familiar sight and are often picked for wine making, to which they give a rich bouquet. Later in the year the elderberries,

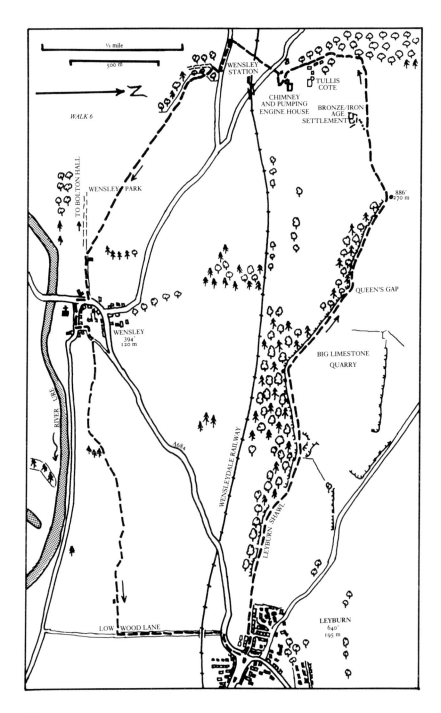

½ mile

500 m

WALK 6

WENSLEY
STATION

TULLIS
COTE

CHIMNEY
AND PUMPING
ENGINE HOUSE

BRONZE/IRON
AGE
SETTLEMENT

TO BOLTON HALL

WENSLEY PARK

886'
270 m

QUEEN'S GAP

WENSLEY
394'
120 m

BIG LIMESTONE
QUARRY

RIVER URE

A684

WENSLEYDALE RAILWAY

LEYBURN SHAWL

LOW WOOD LANE

LEYBURN
640'
195 m

From top: elderberry and blackthorn (sloes).

hunting regularly, under guard, and could easily have reached this point on some occasion.

At the end of the wood, descend through one field to a stile, then diagonally to the far corner of the next. In the lower part of the third field, near Tullis Cote, are the remains of an ancient Bronze Age settlement where a grinding stone and flints have been found, though there is little to be seen now.

Go along the contour across a cart track towards Gillfield Wood. There is a fine view of Penhill from here, showing the typical stepped outline of the Yoredale group of strata with a capping of millstone grit. Turn left down the lane past Tullis Cote Farm. On the right before the farm is the site of Keld Head smelt mill and the beginning of the two mile flue that goes up the fellside to the Cobscar chimney. Visitors on the train were told to look out for the 'two mile long chimney'! This was a very important mining area. The smelt mill has been completely destroyed, but in the mid-nineteenth century it was one of the most advanced ore hearth mills in the country. On the right, a peep through the rowan trees and nettles reveals an attractive waterfall on Wensley Brook.

Follow the course of the stream past the old square chimney stack on the left. This was attached to the large pumping engine house of the great Keld Head leadmine, which was working until 1888. It had a large workforce, and men walked here each day from many of the surrounding villages. It is now surrounded by wild garlic, nettles and red campion. Near the cottages is the site of the older Preston smelt mill which was working before 1700.

Cross the minor road, then the course of the railway. Perhaps the ballast for the railway came from the leadmine spoil heaps, for the lead-tolerant plant, spring sandwort, grows well here; its small white

as well as the sloes, the fruit of the blackthorn, are also used to make good wines.

Part way along the Shawl is Queens Gap where, as legend has it, Mary Queen of Scots was captured after having escaped from Bolton Castle. It is debatable whether she 'escaped', but she was allowed to go flowers are in bloom all summer despite its name. The rail crossing is only a few paces from the old Wensley station, which was closed with the line in March 1954 after only eighty years' use.

A new metal footpath gate leads onto the next road. Turn left here for some 220 yards (200m) and into the wood of tall trees on the right, part of the Bolton estate, where the track carries on to Bolton Hall. Turn off to the left after only fifty yards (50m), to a stile on the edge of the wood and across meadow parkland of the estate, descending to the long drive which has its entrance in Wensley.

Wensley is the lovely quiet village which has the honour of giving its name to the dale. It is so neat and pretty, it might be quite in place in the south of England rather than the Pennine Dales. It has a long history, and was the first market town in Wensleydale when it received its charter in 1202. An outbreak of plague in 1563 was a major disaster for the village and allowed Askrigg and Leyburn to overtake it. From then on Wensley declined as a market centre.

The church, however, a testament to its earlier importance, is quite outstanding and is full of fascinating items. It dates from 1245 and has close connections with the Scrope family of Bolton Castle. But there are signs of an earlier church. A Saxon stone carving refers to Donfrid, priest in 760. There are wall paintings dated 1330 and a fourteenth century memorial brass, thought to be one of the finest in the country. The beautifully-carved choir stalls were made in 1527 by the Ripon school of carvers. A finely carved oak screen, saved from Easby Abbey in Swaledale at the time of the dissolution, surrounds the family box pews of the lords of Bolton. The large wooden box near the door is a reliquary, which may have contained the relics of St Agatha, the patron saint of Easby Abbey.

Wensley Church.

Leave the churchyard at the far corner, cross the road and turn left in front of the white house with the lovely garden. Take the gate on the right at the bend in the road for a path through the fields. The gate is waymarked but it also has a carved inscription: 'P.O.W. Italian 15.5.44'. The path passes through a nature reserve, Old Glebe Field. A Site of Special Scientific Interest, the meadow contains a large variety of flowering plants and is managed by the Yorkshire Wildlife Trust. It is noted particularly for its lovely cowslips and green winged orchids which, if they are not eaten by rabbits, adorn this sloping field in the spring. Later on the purple blooms of betony grow well here. Betony was grown in churchyards to ward off evil spirits, and it was said that if serpents were placed in a ring of betony they would fight to the death. Keep to the wall at the top of this field to experience a variety of old-fashioned squeezer stiles, originally well-built, but not all in good condition today. Without losing height, head for a group of ash trees and pass above a barn until the field path comes out onto Low Wood Lane. Turn left up to the top of the leafy lane, lined with flowers. A right turn brings you back into Leyburn market place.

WALK 7: REDMIRE FORCE FROM WEST WITTON

Start: West Witton. Grid Ref: 063 884
Distance: 6 miles (9½ km)
OS Maps: Outdoor Leisure 30 or Landranger 98 and 99
Walking Time: 3 hours

West Witton is on the main A684 road on the south side of the river, the starting point for this easy walk and with space to park in the roadside parking area just outside the village on its east side. The main aim is to visit Redmire Force on the River Ure, preceded by a pleasant riverside stroll where there is excellent birdwatching. This makes a good family walk.

West Witton is strung out along the main road. The church is dedicated to St Bartholomew and was rebuilt in the nineteenth century, though the tower is sixteenth century. The village was once noted for the dyeing of wool and making of wooden buttertubs. It is a linear village, whose houses were built for lead miners who worked across the valley at Keld Head mine or the smelter there above Wensley Station. Much of the building took place in the early nineteenth century, filling in spaces to make a continuous street. But there are some fine older houses worth a closer look. Catterall Hall is now a hotel but was lived in by the Catterall family for generations. Those houses on the north side of the street have fine views across the valley.

A most interesting tradition of West Witton is the 'Burning of Owd Bartle', which comes on the Saturday nearest to the 24th August, St Bartholomew's Day. It is the climax of West Witton Feast. The custom is so old that its explanation is lost in time, though it is very much a part of the folklore of the dale. An effigy of Bartle is carried down the street with the people crowding round, several stops are made and the following rhyme is chanted by the caller, with cheers from the crowd, before Bartle is taken to a bonfire to be burnt at Grassgill:

'At Penhill Crags he tore his rags;
At Hunters Thorn he blew his horn;
At Capplebank Stee he brak his knee;
At Briskill Beck he brak his neck;
At Wadham's End he couldn't fend;
At Grass Gills End they made his end.
Shout, lads, shout!'

There are several explanations of the custom. Old Bartle could represent St Bartholomew, and it is said that a statue of the saint was saved from the church at the time of the Reformation. But the villagers believe it was a pig thief who stole swine from the monks of Jervaulx and was pursued as described in the rhyme. In connection with this is a story of the giant of Penhill who kept wild boars and had one stolen. Going back further in time, it is possible that Bartle was a fertility figure of the harvest, a sort of corn spirit which rose from the final sheaf. So take your pick. The feast also includes a village show, children's sports and a fell race up Penhill.

Start near the sign 'West Witton' on the main road at the east end of the village. The fingerpost says 'Common Lane 1¼ via Park Gate', and the path starts off fairly close to the road. Field mushrooms grow along here. The round white caps are easily seen, the young 'buttons' having bright pink gills which later turn dark brown.

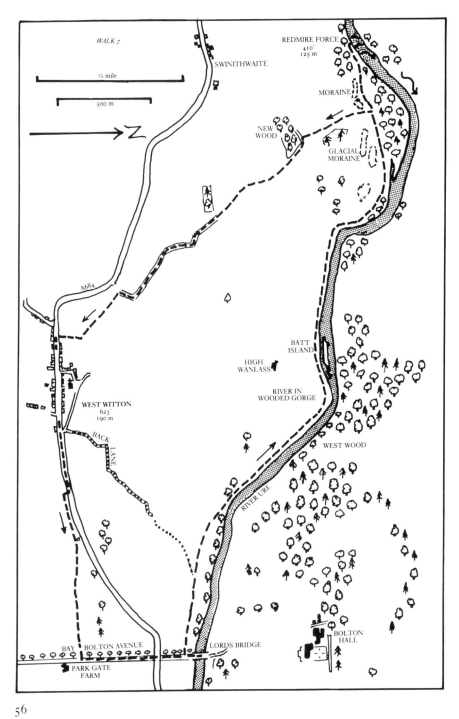

WALK 7

½ mile

500 m

N

SWINITHWAITE

REDMIRE FORCE
410'
125 m

MORAINE

NEW
WOOD

GLACIAL
MORAINE

A684

BATT
ISLAND

HIGH
WANLASS

RIVER IN
WOODED GORGE

WEST WITTON
623'
190 m

BACK
LANE

WEST WOOD

RIVER URE

BAY
BOLTON AVENUE

PARK GATE
FARM

LORDS BRIDGE

BOLTON
HALL

They certainly have more flavour than cultivated ones.

The path passes several small barns to the avenue of mature sycamores just below Park Gate Farm. This is Bay Bolton Avenue and links Bolton Hall with Middleham High Moor. Turn down the hill, crossing the main road by the gatekeeper's cottage to the ornamental Lord's Bridge over the River Ure. Straight ahead is the impressive facade of Bolton Hall, enhancing the wooded parkland that surrounds it. The hall is the private residence of Lord Bolton and is not open to the public, but there are several public footpaths through the grounds.

Treecreeper.

From the bridge, return to the stile and the path which takes you upstream on the left side of the river. After two or three fields, cross the small beck and turn down to the riverside, following the sign 'Hestholme Bridge'. The next part of the walk is along a lovely section of tree-clad riverbank, sometimes high above the water but with some interesting birdlife to look out for. Among the beeches and sycamores you may catch sight of the treecreeper. This small mouse-like bird with a thin curved bill and stiff pointed tail is a climber of tree trunks. It clings to the bark with its feet apart, climbing jerkily in spirals round the trunk or along the underside of a branch.

The great spotted woodpecker is another woodland bird you may catch sight of. Its glossy black and white appearance is offset by bright red under the tail. It is attracted to dead trees, where it breaks away bark by hammering with its sharp bill as it hunts for wood-boring larvae.

Above the river, sand martins twitter in their erratic flight as they catch insects on the wing. Waders include the tail-bobbing common sandpiper, more easily seen in flight when, with stiff bowed wings, it moves with brief flicks and glides, showing its white wing bars. The larger redshank has long red legs – hence its name – and flies fast with jerky shallow beats, tilting to show its more marked white wing bars and white rump. The biggest wader is the curlew, and, although it breeds on upland pastures, it also frequents the river here to feed. Other water birds along this stretch include mallard, pied wagtail and grey wagtail. The handsome Canada goose is fairly common in flocks of twenty or more along the river. This big bird is grey-brown with a glossy black head and neck, a whitish front and a white chinstrap. It was introduced as an ornamental bird from North America during the seventeenth century, and in the last fifty years there has been a rapid increase in numbers.

Pass Batt Island, a small wooded islet in the middle of the river, then through a hummocky landscape and over a ladder stile. Note the cart track to the left here, the return route. Go straight forward to a second ladder stile at the far right corner. The hummocky nature of the land is a relic of the Ice Age, the mounds being remnants

Redshank.

of a lateral moraine left by the Wensleydale glacier. The hillocks consist of debris which is less clayey than that of drumlins, because it collected along the edge of the ice and the finer particles had more chance of being washed out. As a result, the soils are well drained and calcareous, the basis for an interesting flora.

The ladder stile brings you through the woods and down to Redmire Force. This series of small waterfalls is not quite so spectacular or famous as those at Aysgarth, but the falls make a picturesque scene.

They are formed in the Great Scar lime-stone, each step emphasising the bedding of the strata, which is roughly horizontal though here it has a slight tilt in the upstream direction. Blocks of limestone have broken off as the river eroded its bed. It is a very nice spot for a pause, a picnic or a paddle, with the sound of running water and the rustle of the wind in the trees for company.

Half a mile (800m) downstream from here is the site of Redmire Well, a sulphur well which has now dried up. However, in Victorian times it was famous for the healing powers of its water, and lots of people visited the springs to drink the water or take some home with them. Paths were laid out and there was even a stone bath for a full immersion. Nearby there are the remains of an old corn mill which was functioning as early as the fifteenth century.

Return through the woods to the ladder stile and to the cart track which leads away from the river. The route continues along the left side of New Wood and up to a metal gate at the top corner of the field. Follow the wall on the left to the end and into a walled lane. On a corner, before reaching the main road, take the field path to West Witton. A wooden gate leads to a fenced path right into the village, with a chance to inspect it from one end to the other.

WALK 8: PENHILL AND TEMPLARS CHAPEL FROM WEST BURTON

Start: West Burton. Grid Ref 017 866
Distance: 9½ miles (15 km)
OS Maps: Outdoor Leisure 30 or Landranger 98 and 99
Walking time: 4 hours

Here is a full day's walk which includes a steep climb up onto Penhill Crags and Penhill Beacon. There are brilliant views from the top, a descent along the edge of Middleham High Moor, a visit to Templars Chapel and a lovely return walk via Morpeth Gate to West Burton. There is parking by the green.

One of the most attractive of Wensleydale villages, West Burton guards the entrance to Walden and sits on the margin of Bishopdale. It lies off the main roads, and its cottages and houses overlook the large sloping green. Like East Witton, it is the total effect of buildings and green that give it its character. The cottages were once the homes of quarrymen and leadminers, and many of them now provide holiday accommodation. There is a market cross and stocks on the green near to the Fox and Hounds, but the village never had a market. Nor is there a church, which is provided by Aysgarth. West Burton has several footpaths converging on it and is an excellent centre for walkers.

Start at the lower end of the green, and go down to the right past the old woollen mill – now holiday flats – to the attractive packhorse bridge and the waterfalls. What a lovely scene this is, the pretty Cauldron Falls being the focus of a sheltered glade. Walden Beck is eating back and down into its bed, and the position of the waterfall is known as a 'knick point' in the long profile of the river.

Go over the bridge and up the field path to the corner of Barrack Wood. In the spring you will hear the songs of many woodland birds along here as they sing out their territorial claims. These include the wood warbler, which is a little larger than

the willow warbler and has more yellow-green plumage. Its song includes a trill rather like the rapid bounce of a ping pong ball. In May, Barrack Wood is full of bluebells, St John's wort, greater stitchwort, wild garlic and lots of primroses. Pass through a steep field, which in spring is a show of cowslips and violets, and on to Morpeth Gate. On the old 1854 OS map it was called Morphet Gate and, according to Geoffrey Wright, is part of a medieval road leading from Middleham to the lords' hunting forests of Bishopdale.

Keep on up the track as Morpeth Scar (formed by the Middle limestone) comes into view on the right; to the left Morpeth Wood clings to the steep slopes. The lane widens and levels out, and continues as a fine example of a green road, known as High Lane. For the next two miles (3km) the track maintains a constant height and is never less than thirty feet (9m) wide, suggesting a stopping place for drovers to graze their animals. In April and May, early purple orchids abound along here on one section of the track, and the richly-coloured spikes leave one with a lasting impression. The bulk of Penhill comes into view on the right, and the limestone cliffs of Dove Scar (the Main limestone) and Low Dove Scar (the Underset limestone) below it.

Two walled lanes come in from the left;

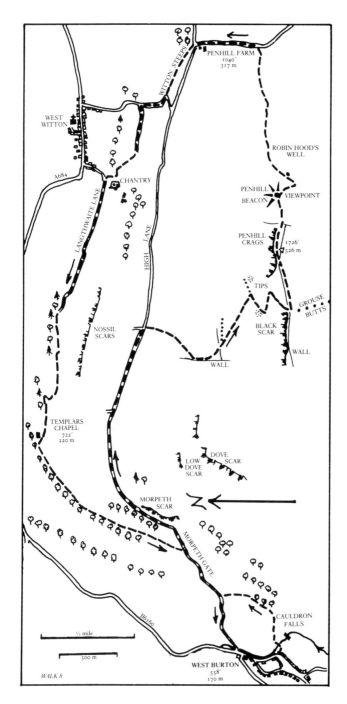

WEST
WITTON

A684

WITTON STEEPS

PENHILL FARM
1040'
317 m

ROBIN HOOD'S
WELL

CHANTRY

PENHILL
BEACON · VIEWPOINT

LANGTHWAITE LANE

HIGH LANE

PENHILL
CRAGS 1726'
526 m

TIPS

NOSSIL
SCARS

GROUSE
BUTTS

BLACK
SCAR

WALL

WALL

TEMPLARS
CHAPEL
722'
220 m

DOVE
SCAR

LOW
DOVE
SCAR

MORPETH
SCAR

MORPETH GATE

CAULDRON
FALLS

B6160

½ mile

500 m

WALK 8

WEST BURTON
558'
170 m

60

Cauldron Falls.

opposite the second one, take the footpath to the right, signposted 'Black Scar'. The path is a well-engineered miners' track, which winds gradually uphill through the last gate to open rough-grazing land below Black Scar. At this point the well-worn green path continues parallel to the wall. It is here you must fork right on a less distinct path and aim for the top end of the second broken-down wall. Pick up another miners' track and turn right to the top of the westernmost spoil heap (the one on the right, now grassed over). The deeply incised path then winds up the steep escarpment to the left of Black Scar, and emerges

through a gap in the wall onto the edge of Penhill. You suddenly come out onto a heather moor with the first of a line of shooting butts straight ahead. The deeply worn track in fact carries on through the heather and must be an old peat road.

Turn left along the wall, soon crossing the stile to Penhill Crags. From here there are magnificent views of upper Wensleydale to the left, and the rest of the dale stretches out before you with Darlington in the distance.

The gritstone crags are the haunt of ravens and peregrines. The raven is the largest of the crows and can be recognised by its powerful, slow wing beats, the swept-back 'hands' of its primary feathers and its deep, grunting 'prruk prruk'. The peregrine is a smaller bird. It is blue-grey above, has black moustaches and is barred paler below. Its broad wings are pointed and the tail is long and tapered. The peregrines mate for life, and often return year after year to the same eyrie.

A little further on is Penhill Beacon, and the view on a clear day takes in not only the length of Wensleydale but also the North Yorkshire Moors. The beacon, 1,685 feet (514m) above sea level, is a very popular place for a walk either from the nearby road or from further afield. It is one of a series of beacons across England where fires were lit to transmit the news of a national celebration or disaster. It also marks the possible burial place of an Iron Age chieftain. The site may be the source of the legend of the giant of Penhill, descendant of the god Thor. This is one of the best of all the old tales, a long story which ends with the wicked giant falling to his death from the crags. The precipitous cliffs of both Black Scar and Penhill Crags are due to landslips which were active at one time, and which have left the steep scars and the hummocky ground below them.

From the beacon, walk round to the track past Robin Hood's Well, a natural spring in the hillside, and through several gates to the road. Go down the road for a third of a mile (500m) to Penhill Farm, with Middleham High Moor on the right, where the training gallops are used by the race horses in the summer months. At the road junction, cross over to a path which leads down the sloping hillside to the left, known as Witton Steeps. Growing here in the spring are wood anemones of a wide variety of colours, from pure white to deep pink. Orchids include the common spotted, a deep pink compact flower, and early purple, which has a longer, less compact

flower head. The latter's common name of cock flower refers to the root tubers, which look like a pair of testicles.

The path comes out at a hairpin bend on the road. After 200 yards (180m) down the road, turn left onto Watery Lane. In early summer the roadside verge is covered in a mass of yellow crosswort, one of the bedstraws. It has yellowish-green leaves and tiny yellow flowers. Both the leaves and the flowers are in fours, making a cross. The lane, living up to its name, can be very wet and may be avoided by using a parallel path in the fields alongside. However, it soon becomes drier and more attractive, with hawthorn and the rare field maple.

After the two barns, go diagonally across the field, through the Chantry caravan site and down through the wood – in May full of bluebells. You are now very near to West Witton, and the name Chantry reminds us that the monks of Jervaulx had a chapel here.

Turn up the hill away from the village and onto Langthwaite Lane, signposted 'Templars Ch 1'. This green lane, being high on the side of the valley, has striking views across Wensleydale. A rookery high in the sycamores is followed by the old hedgerow favourites of hawthorn, wild rose, blackthorn, gooseberry and holly. The blackthorn almost fills the lane for a stretch. In March its blossom is spectacular, but the sloes are not really ready for picking until the end of October, when they are destined for making wine or sloe gin.

At the end of the lane, go through the fields and drop down to a lower level between two woods to Templars Chapel, otherwise described as Penhill Preceptory. Not much remains of the place, which once included a chapel and residential buildings run by the Knights Templar for travellers to the Holy Land, built about the year 1200. The small stone coffins in the chapel ruins are the most interesting of the

Templars Chapel.

remains. They are too short for a full-grown Crusader, so bodies may have been buried with the limbs folded beneath them.

Follow the footpath to Morpeth Gate above the woods. Several springs have their source along here, as water drains from the base of the limestone above, to pass over impermeable strata. The view ahead shows both Walden and Bishopdale valleys stretching into the distance with Wasset Fell between them, and West Burton nestled at the foot of the fell and apparently in neither dale.

Go down the lane of Morpeth Gate, this time going right down to the fine packhorse bridge over Walden Beck and round by the road to West Burton and the complete circuit. Along the lane grow a mass of the tiny pink stars of shining cranesbill, identified by its glossy green leaves.

WALK 9: WALDEN FROM WEST BURTON

Start: West Burton. Grid Ref: 017 866
Distance: 6½ miles (10½ km)
OS Maps: Outdoor Leisure 30 or Landranger 98
Walking Time: 3 hours

This makes a delightful walk in a very quiet area with a variety of landscapes. From West Burton, it visits the hamlet of Newbiggin in Bishopdale before crossing over, through the conifers, back into Walden, a lovely dale and especially good for birdwatchers. West Burton is just off the B6160 from Wharfedale and lies not far from Aysgarth Falls. Parking alongside the green.

A popular holiday village, but one with a daily life of its own, West Burton has the attraction of being off the main road and not on a through road to anywhere. From the village there is a road to the north side of Walden and one to the south, each being a cul-de-sac. West Burton may not have such an ancient look about it, but it was listed in the *Domesday Book*. There are two fine eighteenth century houses but most of the cottages are younger than this, having been built for miners and quarrymen. The long green has a cross like a church spire on a flight of steps, with the stocks next to it.

Walk up to the highest part of the village, known as Town Head, and turn off to the right through the metal gate and left at the bottom of the second field. This takes you in the direction of Newbiggin through several fields and on to a lovely lane. There is a scattering of field barns, and many ancient hedges with mature ash, sycamore and oak trees growing out of them. The age of a hedge can be estimated by the number of trees and shrubs growing in it: the greater the number of species, the older the hedge. It is this kind of old farmland which the redstart and willow warbler return to each spring, and which is the ideal home for residents such as the wren, robin and song thrush. The perky little wren is our most common bird, with 10,000,000

Wren.

64

Walden and Penhill.

breeding pairs in Britain. It is well suited for foraging amongst undergrowth and along hedgerows, but has a wide distribution in the Dales and can be found high on the fell tops in the drystone walls and rocky places.

The cobbled, tree-lined lane brings you out into Newbiggin – meaning new buildings – and it is worth a stroll through the village. Halfway along is a pretty waterfall as Mill Beck descends to road level, and on its left is an old sheep-fold and sheep-wash. There are several restored old barns and cottages, many of which were homes of leadminers; a miners's track leaves the end of the village for Wasset Fell.

Return to the beginning of the village to the point where the lane goes off to the left, and here go up the hillside between two walls. Curve to the left and cross a small stream, which you should then follow up the hillside to the conifer plantation ahead. Turn up alongside the plantation for a few yards to a wooden stile which takes you into the wood.

The conifers – mainly spruce – here make an abrupt change to one's surroundings. Such plantations on the fells have been criticised for producing a desert for wildlife. Soon after planting, when the land is fenced off from sheep, the grasses grow well and this encourages small mammals like the field vole, which in turn attract owls and kestrels. Small conifer trees provide good nesting for many small birds such as chaffinch, whinchat, goldcrest and tits. However, when mature, like these sitka spruce, the trees grow so close

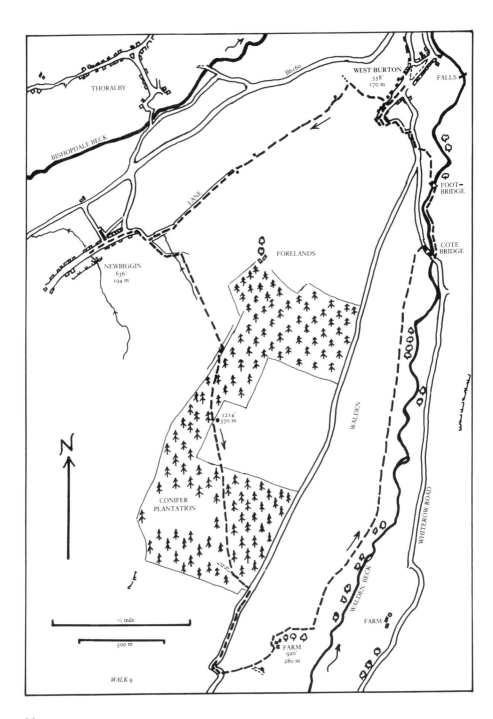

THORALBY

B6160

WEST BURTON
558′
170 m

FALLS

BISHOPDALE BECK

LANE

FOOT-
BRIDGE

COTE
BRIDGE

FORELANDS

NEWBIGGIN
636′
194 m

WALDEN

1214′
370 m

CONIFER
PLANTATION

WHITEROW ROAD

WALDEN BECK

N

½ mile

500 m

FARM

FARM
920′
280 m

WALK 9

66

together that they exclude the light and, except for a few fungi, there is no undergrowth. The pine needles are acid, and even worms and snails become rare. When the timber is felled the whole process may begin again with new plantings.

Proceed to a stretch of open grassland with rushes and molehills. Continue in the same direction and enter the wood again, by a ladder stile between larches and spruce. The path can be muddy in the winter and in the autumn there are fairy rings of toadstools under the trees. Foxes use the trail, as indicated by the droppings. These often contain fur, feather and bone fragments, and break into pieces – you can tell them by the twisted point at one end and the greyish colour.

Turn right at the road for a third of a mile (500m), then left onto a farm track for the return down the delightful dale of Walden. The name, meaning woods, refers to the whole dale – you never say Waldendale! This lonely valley was even isolated during the Ice Age, when it escaped having its own glacier, and as a result is a water-worn, steep V-shape, in contrast to the broad U-shape of Bishopdale. In the fourteenth century, when it was the haunt of red deer, it was made a hunting reserve along with Bishopdale and Penhill. Until the early part of the nineteenth century, Walden was a refuge of the wild cat; the pine marten declined here only after the 1850s. Today it is an ESA (Environmentally Sensitive Area), where farming methods are designed to encourage the growth of wild flowers and therefore butterflies and birds.

Down the farm track, take the left fork to Cowstone Gill Farm. Keep to the left of the farm, cross the wooded gill, and descend to where the path keeps much the same height above Walden Beck on its way down the dale to the road and Cote Bridge. From the end of April the cuckoo makes its familiar

sound, though is much less seen. The female eats one egg of the foster parent – usually a meadow pipit – and lays one to replace it. It may lay a dozen eggs or more, all in different nests of the same species. When hatched, the young naked cuckoo pushes out the other eggs and soon grows too big for the nest. Besides the grey wagtail and the common sandpiper, the beck attracts the grey heron, which knows where there is good fishing to be had. Besides fish it will also take frogs or small mammals, standing motionless and making a lightning stab at its prey.

In the autumn, hundreds of fieldfares flock between the clumps of trees and the open fields, often accompanied by the smaller redwings. These birds are winter visitors from Scandinavia, both are of the thrush/blackbird family and both have a speckled breast. The fieldfare, a large thrush 10 inches (25cm) long, has a grey head and rump, whereas the dark brown redwing is smaller, being only 8 inches (20cm) long. The rich red colour under the wing of the redwing shows up in flight, but only a small patch of red on the flanks is visible when the bird is resting.

Where there are many small birds the sparrowhawk is not far away. It haunts the edge of woodland and hedgerows at low level, but if seen soaring and diving in the breeding season, the distinctive short, rounded wings and long tail – spread or closed – may help to identify it.

At the road, turn right down to the bridge, then along the right bank close to the river, to cross the footbridge and up the fields to the road, here known as Dame Lane. Turn right for a few yards, then left with the sign 'Town Head 200 yards'. From here you look down on the rooftops of West Burton, which is expanding up the hill. In the distance the lead smelt mill chimney of Cobscar shows up on the horizon.

WALK 10: AYSGARTH FALLS AND BOLTON CASTLE

Start: Aysgarth Falls, National Park Visitor Centre. Grid Ref: 011 888
Distance: 7 miles (11½ km)
OS Maps: Outdoor Leisure 30 or Landranger 98
Walking Time: 4 hours

This walk is likely to become a classic. It is one of the walks published by the National Park and visits two of the the most popular tourist attractions in Wensleydale, Aysgarth Falls and Bolton Castle. It is very pleasant walking, the views from higher up are magnificent, and the birds and flowers exceptional. Park at the National Park centre.

From the National Park visitor centre, go by the footpath down the road and cross over into Freeholders' Wood to visit Aysgarth Falls. The wood was purchased by the National Park because of the large number of visitors. There are twenty-nine houses in Carperby which have the ancient right of 'estovers' – to gather sticks in the wood between November and March. The National Park has restarted coppicing of the woodland after a gap of eighty years, and the twenty-nine lucky households now have their firewood delivered! Coppicing entails cutting back trees to ground level every seven to twenty years and allowing a cluster of shoots to grow. In this way trees will go on for ever. It is possible to coppice all trees except silver birch and conifers. These days very few woods are managed in this way, but the system does provide plenty of light for flowering plants as well as thick cover for birds. Newly-coppiced trees have to be protected against nibbling rabbits and roe deer. The dominant tree in Freeholder's Wood is hazel, though there are birch, bird cherry, hawthorn and others. The silver birch is a graceful tree with a white bark and long slender twigs. The rounded, pointed leaves have double toothed edges rather like hazel, though the latter are heart-shaped and larger.

The flowers of this primary woodland are particularly varied. Where primroses

and cowslips grow together, you may find the hybrid false oxlip which has primrose flowers on a cowslip stem. Another hybrid is the cross between yellow wood avens and pink water avens. The result is a yellow drooping flower without a name. A rare plant which grows somewhere hidden in the wood is herb Paris, a sign of an ancient woodland since it does not survive grazing. It is a distinctive plant, with a whorl of four or five leaves and a central green flower.

Visit the middle falls and get a splendid view from a specially-built platform. The rushing waters pour over a sixteen foot (5m) high step of solid Great Scar limestone, with smaller steps beneath of thinner beds of rock. This waterfall is spectacular when the river is in spate.

Along the path to the lower falls grow three 'wood' flowers – wood sanicle, wood cranesbill and wood avens – as well as bluebells, goldilocks, wild arum and yellow pimpernel. The tufts of lime-green grass that border the path are wood melick, with its dainty grass head. It is one of the few grasses that grows well in a woodland habitat.

The lower falls can first be viewed from above, and further on reached by a short scramble down to the big slabs of limestone that border the river. If you look carefully at the rock you will discover brachiopod shells and fossil colonies of the coral litho-

68

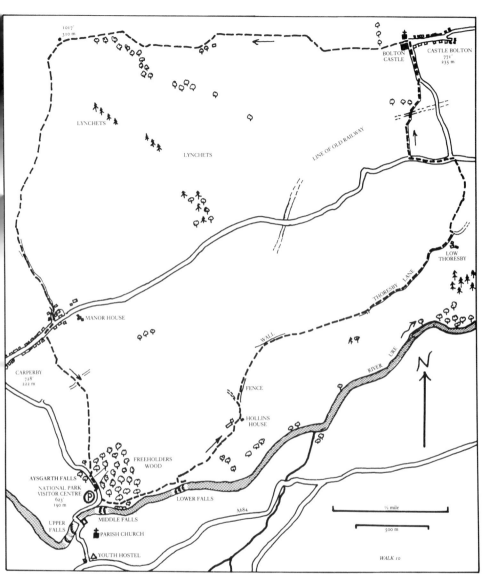

strotion. A few paces from the foot of the 'scramble' is a particularly large colony, five feet (1 · 5 m) across. The succession of falls brings the waters of the Ure down a twenty-six foot (8m) staircase, again in Great Scar limestone. Go up above the falls, where at low water you can see dozens of 'potholes' in the river bedrock, worn by swirling and grinding pebbles. In some places the river has dissolved a way through to a lower bedding plane, ever trying to lower its bed. Along the wet banks here you may find the

Birdseye primrose.

beautiful flowers of butterwort and birdseye primrose, two rather special flowers. Butterwort eats insects by trapping flies in its sticky leaves and has a single purple flower; the pretty pink birdseye

primrose now only grows in the three English counties of Yorkshire, Cumbria and Durham.

Retreat from river level by the same way to the path and back to the stile. Follow the sign to the village of Castle Bolton through the fields. In the spring and early summer you will see a profusion of flowers here, including celandines, primroses and bluebells.

A stile at the end of a wooden fence takes you on to Hollins House Farm. Turn soon, off the farm track, to the right along a wire fence and through large water meadows. There is a new vista across the valley to Bolton Castle, which dominates this part of Wensleydale. The damp, open grassland is the breeding place of lapwing, curlew, redshank and snipe. The lapwing is a large member of the plover family, with a long wispy crest. In flight it has a distinctively floppy beat of its broad, rounded wings and, out of the breeding season, numbers of them form rather straggling parties. In contrast the bigger curlew has a much more leisurely and direct flight, whereas the redshank flies with a nervous, erratic movement with jerky, shallow wing beats. Snipe are more likely to be seen 'drumming' on a summer's evening as they slide through the air.

Pass two metal gates and a stile to reach Thoresby Lane. There is no grazing here, so the plant life has blossomed accordingly. Hawthorn, hazel, holly, blackthorn and wild roses line the route, and in a wet place there are butterbur, watercress, kingcups and meadowsweet. Along the side of the lane grow a mass of wild flowers: cow parsley, St John's wort, goosegrass, crosswort, greater stitchwort, speedwell, tufted vetch, garlic mustard and wood avens. Then further along are water avens, meadowsweet, red campion, bluebell, wood cranesbill, giant bellflower and near the farm white deadnettle.

Bolton Castle.

On the right of the lane, near the river, is the site of the lost village of Thoresby which may have been wiped out by the plague. The name is Danish meaning 'Thor's village', and it was certainly in good shape until the fourteenth century and was named in the *Domesday Book*. Today there are a few mounds which suggest a street of dwellings and a church.

Join the road at Low Thoresby Farm and, after some fifty yards (50m), turn off by a footbridge, over a broken wall, then right through a narrow meadow and another field to the road, ignoring the cart track. Walk left along the road for 320 yards (300m), then right along a bushy path bor-

dered by garlic mustard and white dead-nettle. Having crossed the line of the old railway, you come out just below Bolton Castle.

This amazing building dates from the fourteenth century, when it was the home of the nationally renowned Scrope family. It was built by Richard, Lord Scrope who was Chancellor of England in 1378. Some 200 years later, Mary Queen of Scots was imprisoned here for six months in 1568. She was twenty-six years old, well-educated and had a lively personality. She lived well with a retinue of forty servants, many of whom had to live in the village. She had her rooms in the south-west tower, which you can see today, and went hunting regularly in the surrounding forests. For Mary it was the beginning of nineteen years of captivity in various places under Elizabeth before she was beheaded. Seventy-five years later, during the Civil War, the castle was a royalist stronghold and under siege, but following defeat in November 1645 it was partly destroyed to render it unusable. The impressive structure of the castle, owned by a descendant of Richard, Lord Scrope, is open to visitors and contains some very good displays, with furnished rooms, colourful scenes with lighting and sound effects to bring the past to life, a dungeon, a tea room and five floors to wander through. There is a fantastic view from the castle roof, from where you can see the whole of Wensleydale. In January 1991 the castle won a £650,000 repair grant from English Heritage to make it safe and to open up more of it to visitors.

Go round the castle past the parish church of St Oswald, where exhibitions of local and historical interest are held, through the gate to follow a double track and through three metal gates to more open pastures. Across the dale you can see the high gritstone scarps of Penhill and the valleys of Bishopdale and Walden, and down the dale there is a brilliant view stretching to the distant North Yorkshire Moors. Between Castle Bolton and Carperby are some well-preserved lynchets, the terraces of 700 years of cultivation.

The path descends to join a walled lane and into Carperby. This attractive village has a long main street with a small green, where there is an ancient market cross dated 1674. The founder of the Quakers, George Fox, once preached here, though now the large Quaker meeting house as well as the nearby Methodist chapel are both private houses. Swallows, house martins and swifts are all to be seen here, and the fullness of summer is only complete when you hear the exciting sound of swifts screaming and swooping in a frenzy above the village. When swifts are feeding their young, they catch several hundred small flies on the wing which they mould into a ball at the back of the mouth to take to the nest under the eves of a house. Most of the year they are entirely airborne, eating, drinking, sleeping and even copulating on the wing.

Go as far as the Wheatsheaf and turn left through the fields back to Aysgarth Falls. The route finishes with a second visit to Freeholders' Wood. Cross the track and bear right to reach the road. Pass under the railway bridge to return to the National Park visitor centre.

WALK 11: AYSGARTH, GAYLE ING AND THORALBY

Start: Aysgarth village. Grid Ref: 003 884
Distance: 9 miles (14km)
OS Maps: Outdoor Leisure 30 or Landranger 98
Walking Time: 4½ hours

Starting at Aysgarth village, the walk follows a green lane past Castle Dykes henge, onto open moors, descends to Thoralby in Bishopdale, and ends with a south bank view of the lower falls and a visit to Aysgarth church. The walk is pleasant going and not too rough higher up. It makes a full day's outing. There is limited parking along the road in Aysgarth.

The village of Aysgarth has become well-known because of the famous Aysgarth Falls nearby. It is a busy little community, straddling the main road and popular with visitors. Although it is of Norman foundation and mentioned in the *Domesday Book*, the houses are mainly nineteenth century and there is little that is very old. There is a small green with stocks, but the church is half a mile away above the falls. The Palmer Flatt Hotel is built on the site of a hospice for palmers or crusaders seeking alms. You can buy local cheeses in the village and there is a good pottery here too.

Start off by taking the minor road in the direction of Thornton Rust for a distance of 550 yards (600m). From the road there are good views up the dale. Turn left along the green lane signed 'Gayle Ing 2¼' through Aysgarth Pasture, where there are distinctive signs of life of the high moor. Curlews arrive here in February in their search for nesting sites, and are soon joined by lapwings, redshanks and meadow pipits, all of which enjoy the quiet rough grazing land which stretches from here, uninterrupted except for stone walls, for six miles (10km) over to Langstrothdale. The heartening call of the curlew and the musical whistle of the redshank may accompany you on your way, while the lapwing carries on its antics in the air. There seems to be a

high population of carrion crows here too, not the most favourite of birds as they are notorious egg thieves. They adapt to any habitat and are just as much at home in the city as on the fells.

Soon you will cross the footpath from Thoralby to Thornton Rust, marked by a series of stiles as it crosses Flout Moor Lane at an angle. Then beyond a gate on the left is a view of the mysterious Castle Dykes henge. From the lane you can only see a green hump and a low ridge among the rushes 160 yards (150m) away, so go and have a closer look. A circular ridge, seventy yards (65m) across, encloses a ditch and a round platform in the centre. Instead of standing stones like those of Stonehenge, there were wooden posts which formed a circle on the inner platform. It was a sacred place where fertility rites and other ceremonies took place. Onlookers could stand on the outer bank and view the proceedings from there. It dates from the Neolithic Age and may have been used into the Bronze Age (2000 BC). Henges are not very common, though Yorkshire has the biggest number of them, with several near Ripon and one near Grassington in Wharfedale.

Haw Beck is forded at a bend in the lane, and at the end of the walled road you should go forward and through a gap in the wall (on the left), and turn right again to

73

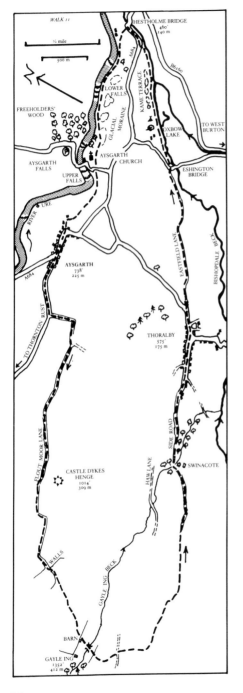

continue in the same direction. Follow the tractor tracks up the hill through the bobbing heads of hare's tail cotton grass to a barn and stile. On the right is the lonely, still-inhabited cottage of Gayle Ing, 1,345 feet (410m) above sea level and two miles (3km) from the nearest metalled road. Below the house is the wooded gill where the small Gayle Ing Beck flows in a large, deep valley, a former meltwater channel that has cut deep into the hillside.

Go forward from the stile, cross the beck by a footbridge and climb up the other side to a small gate. Before you scale the steep slope, and just beyond a gap in a wall, there is a wet patch worth further attention. Growing here in May and June are marsh valerian, scurvygrass, birdseye primrose, butterwort and opposite-leaved golden saxifrage, a wonderful collection of water-loving plants. Birdseye primrose is not as common as it used to be, but its small bright pink flowers are a joy to see. So too are the lovely purple heads of butterwort springing from bright green rosettes of sticky, fly-catching leaves. Golden saxifrage sounds very grand, but don't expect too much: this is a flower without petals, but it does produce a gold-spangled, pale green mat where there is plenty of water about.

From the little gate, go straight forward through the heather and bilberry, then curve round to the left, crossing a cart track known as Stake Road. Eventually the path gets nearer to a wall on the left and passes through a gate. From here there is a new and panoramic view into Bishopdale, both up the dale and down, with the meandering Bishopdale Beck in the bottom and Penhill in the distance. The ice scoured deeply into Bishopdale, forming its U-shaped valley, and that is why the beck runs so sluggishly. The valley floor is lower than that of Wensleydale, which has to descend Aysarth Falls before it reaches the right level to be joined by Bishopdale Beck.

The path is not so easy to find, but crosses the next field to a wall on the right and an iron gate. Look out for the finger posts, 'BW Thoralby', and cross Skellicks Beck to join a double track down the hill to Thoralby. The view of lower Bishopdale is refreshing, for instead of stone walls there is a pattern of hedges round the fields and numbers of trees that make the dale look more fertile and attractive. Lining the track there are many flowers which add colour to the verges, and include yellowrattle, pink herb robert and blue germander speedwell.

A wood on the right is the habitat of nuthatch, chiffchaff, willow warbler and other woodland birds. The song of the chiffchaff is so different from the wistful tune of the willow warbler that, if you did not know, you would expect to see two quite different birds. In appearance they are so alike that only only an expert can tell them apart! The chiffchaff is one of the earliest summer visitors to arrive, and by the last week of March will find a high perch to deliver its monotonous call and stake out its territory. Just past this wood is a patch of damp ground, quite different from that at Gayle Ing, but a place for several wet-loving plants, for here among others grows ragged robin, the bright pink flowers of which are striking. The petals are divided into four thin wisps which gives the flower its name. You may see green-veined white butterflies visiting them for the nectar. In former times a girl would pick a few buds, each representing a boyfriend. The flower that opened first was the one she would marry.

The track descends past the Old Hall into Thoralby, a community with a post office, the George Inn, village hall and Methodist chapel. There are some interesting old houses with dates of 1641, 1653 and 1704 which give the village a quiet, unspoilt charm of times long past. A story

Ragged robin.

of buried treasure is linked to the house dated 1704 and concerns a black teapot filled with gold sovereigns hidden under the floor.

Continue the walk along Eastfield Lane past several old ash trees, lynchets and flowery meadows to Eshington Bridge. From here take the path signed 'Hestholme Bridge' through the campsite and past several mounds, known as 'kames'. These are made up of gravels deposited by floodwaters in crevasses within the melting ice. The pebbles are more rounded that those in drumlins and, being water-sorted, the finer clay is washed out and they are deposited in layers.

Lower Aysgarth Falls.

Join the road for 280 yards (250m), then just before Hestholme Bridge take the path to the left across a field to the riverside. Note the mounds of lateral moraine and the gorge below Aysgarth Falls where the river runs on bedrock. Views of the falls are somewhat obscured by trees from this side of the river and the path remains a little distant from the bank.

The walk continues to the church, which is well worth a visit. The ancient parish used to be the largest in England and included all of upper Wensleydale. The church of St Andrews stands high above the falls in a large churchyard. The beautiful rood screen, painted red, green and gold, is thought to be the work of the Ripon carvers (c1506) – like the pews with their finely carved heads – and both were taken from Jervaulx at the dissolution. The church was rebuilt in Victorian times and retains little of its twelfth century foundation.

The path carries on from the church across the road and through a series of neat stiles along the parishoners' way back to the village of Aysgarth.

WALK 12: ASKRIGG FROM AYSGARTH FALLS

Start: Aysgarth Falls, National Park Visitor Centre. Grid Ref: 011 888
Distance: 10 miles (16km)
OS Maps: Outdoor Leisure 30 or Landranger 98
Walking Time: 5 hours

A visit is first made to the old village of Carperby, then the cliffs of Ivy Scar beckon the walker along a lovely trail high up on the side of the valley to the beautiful old dales village of Askrigg. The return route takes in the line of the former railway and the banks of the River Ure. This is a full day's excursion, but is easy walking with magnificent views and a wide variety of interest on the way. There is a spacious car park at the visitor centre.

The road bridge at Aysgarth Falls was once a packhorse bridge. It was widened in 1784 and from it there is an excellent view of the upper falls. Also in 1784, Yore Mill was built for wool spinning. It was a large mill, the water power of which was later used for cotton spinning, and the grinding of corn. After being burnt down it was rebuilt in 1853, twice as big and five storeys high. So much stock was produced that thousands of jerseys were exported to Italy as 'red shirts' for Garibaldi's army. It is now occupied by the Yorkshire Museum of Carriages and Horse Drawn Vehicles, which takes you back to the age before the motor car. At the top of the hill, Aysgarth Falls has its church, hotel and youth hostel.

The walk starts from the National Park visitor centre, where there are displays and publications on the area. At the far end of the car park, go up the steps and over the embankment of the old railway. The path runs parallel to the road, which it joins for 100 yards (90m). Just past the road junction it passes through the field, a metal gate and to the right of the farmyard, and up into Carperby. This linear village is strung out along the road which runs from Askrigg to Redmire. As the *by* suggests, Carperby was first settled by Danes and today has some attractive houses, farms and village green. It was one of the earliest villages in

the dale to obtain a market charter, which it received in 1305, and the stepped market cross dates from 1674. One of the two Wesleyan chapels and the tall Quaker meeting house are now private dwellings. This is where the Wensleydale breed of sheep originated in 1838. Once known as 'mugs', these large sheep have wool down to the ground and are mainly used for cross-breeding.

Go left through the village, past Matthews Well and the market cross, and turn right at the end. Beyond the two walls, bear left to a stile and continue up the hill on the left of the wall on a cart track, to reach Carperby stone mine. The high-grade flagstone, used for slating roofs, was quarried by tunnelling into the hillside. Since the flagstone is overlain by the thick Hardraw limestone, the underground quarry avoided the removal of large amounts of limestone rock in the process.

Turn left through the heaps of flagstone in the up-dale direction through two gates and onto Ox Close, a fine, open situation with the great limestone cliff of Ivy Scar on the right, the strata dipping as steeply as anywhere in the dale. Magnificent views across to the contrasting flat tops of Addlebrough, Wether Fell and Dodd Fell reflect the horizontal nature of the bulk of Wensleydale rocks. Curlews and lapwings

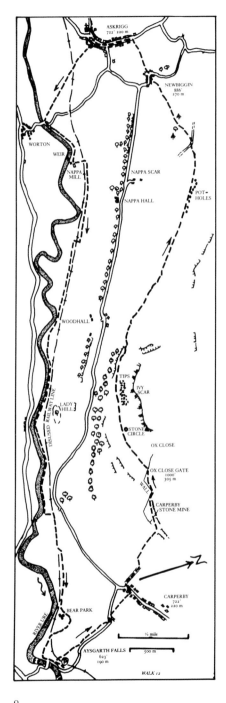

are all around, and in early June you will see the yellow mountain pansy scattered about these pastures. It is a plant that grows best on the leached reddish soils of this classic locality. Not far along the path, you can study the biggest stone circle in the Yorkshire dales. It measures thirty yards (28m) across – though is not quite a true circle – and is made up of sixteen stones with other stones in the centre. Stones from many circles have been taken for gate posts or for use in drystone walls, but this one stands almost complete and is typical of the Bronze Age.

The next big attraction are the tip heaps of Wet Groves Mine at the foot of Ivy Scar. A rich vein was worked here and the tips are rewarding for a variety of minerals. Barite is the only really heavy white mineral, and you only need to weigh a lump in the hand to identify it. Fluorite is more watery looking, heavyish and sometimes shows the crystal faces of a cube. Calcite is white and breaks to form a rhomb shape (like a deformed cube). These three white minerals were thrown out by the miners as waste, so are easy to find. Galena, the ore of lead, is a dull grey until freshly broken when it shines like silver, and again can be identified by hefting it in the hand as it is the heaviest of the common minerals. You may also find sphalerite, the ore of zinc which is a greasy dark brown colour and heavy. Hydrozincite occurs too, and bright green specks of the copper mineral malachite are also present.

A little further on, the path continues along the top of the Hardraw limestone. There are more mountain pansies but also a profusion of rockroses, and at the end of this scarp is a ford through the infant Eller Beck where thrift, spring sandwort and scurvygrass grow. The bright yellow five-petalled rockrose is the most delicate of flowers. The plant is a trailing, almost evergreen perennial with narrow pairs of

Addlebrough from Askrigg. The line of trees marks the scar of Hardraw limestone.

leaves. It is strange to find thrift so far from the sea, for the 'sea pink' – although rare in Wensleydale – is common just a few hundred yards lower down Eller Beck, where the roadside becomes a carpet of pink in the summer. The name of this beautiful flower relates to how the plant thrives, even in poor soils, where long roots reach deep down for moisture. Spring sandwort grows among the thrift and you probably noticed it on the tip heaps of the leadmine. This delicate little white flower is also known as leadwort as it is most common near where lead is mined.

Minerals (clockwise from top left): barite, galena, calcite and fluorite.

From the ford, follow the track through a gate on the left, and turn right onto another cart track and up the hill. Pass a line of shake holes and enter a green lane which is joined by a road from the left. In fifty yards (50m) turn through a stile on the left to cross a field and a small wood. The views from the footpath as it approaches Ellerkin Scar are magnificent. You can see the Roman road on the other side of the dale where it climbs and disappears over Wether Fell to Ingleton and, straight across, the tree-lined scar is the Hardraw limestone with the village of Thornton Rust at its left hand end and Worton low down near the river.

From the wood, go through the fields to Newbiggin, over the stone bridge, along a lane for a short distance and left over a stile.

The path leads through the flowery fields of Stony Bank, with a bird's-eye view of Askrigg situated between two small hills before you drop down into the village. This lovely village sits on the sunny, south-facing slopes of the dale. It has a long history dating from Norman times but became important in the seventeenth and eighteenth centuries, when it was the main market town for upper Wensleydale. There are some stately old houses of the same period. The main street winds down the hill among prosperous buildings to the market square, where the stepped cross, cobbles and bull ring are reminders of the past. Trades that flourished here included dyeing, hand-knitting, clock making, brewing, spinning and leadmining. The story of Askrigg is told in the local history classic

Yorkshire Village by Marie Hartley and Joan Ingilby, who still live in the village. Near the cross is the imposing Skeldale House of James Herriot's television story, *All Creatures Great and Small.* Standing in a fine position overlooking the square, St Oswald's Church is the biggest in the dale. It is of twelfth century foundation, has a fifteenth century tower and sixteenth century aisles.

Dragging yourself away from this fascinating village, take the route opposite the market cross through the cottages and signed 'Aysgarth 4½'. Turn right, then right again at the branching of footpaths to cross the old railway and down to the floodplain where a paved path leads to Worton. Askrigg Bottoms is the home of oystercatcher, redshank and lapwing, and along the river from Worton Bridge live reed bunting and sandpiper. Reed buntings like the riverside where they can find the cover of a few bushes or trees. The male is easily recognised by its black head and white collar, the female being a rather drab brown. It has a low, jerky flight and may be seen perching on a wire fence voicing its indifferent song. The redstart is another bird which likes a bit of cover, and you are quite likely to see this handsome bird on the next part of the walk, its fiery chestnut tail being most conspicuous.

At Nappa Mill, go left up the lane and onto the railway embankment, and then through fields between river and railway. After years of delay and to the accompaniment of flags and fireworks, the line from Leyburn to Askrigg was finally opened on the 1st February 1877, and the last section to Hawes in May 1878. The new railway provided a valuable and comfortable means of travel and improved access for visitors to the dale. Instead of slow progress over bumpy roads, goods trains were able to carry quarried stone, wool, livestock and fresh milk out of the dale, with coal, building materials, provisions and manufactured goods coming in to boost the economy. The last passenger train ran in April 1954; the track was removed above Redmire in 1965.

Where the river bends near to the line of the railway, sand martins have taken up nest holes in the bank, and their chattering can be heard as they swoop and dive over the water. The path continues alongside the river and passes Lady Hill on the left, a perfectly-shaped drumlin with a dozen pine trees on its crest. Although Lady Hill has a rock core, during the Ice Age it was plastered with boulder clay, and smoothed beneath the ice into its present shape. The river is rather still in this section, which the sand martins, coots and Canada geese seem to prefer.

At the footbridge, take the 'Aysgarth Falls' path to the railway. After a short distance on the railway, the path runs along the left of it, up the hill then round Bear Park Farm, where isolated copper beeches, red flowering horse chestnuts and pines make a parkland scene. Cross the old railway down to the upper falls and the path to the road bridge. From here a footpath leads back to the National Park visitor centre.

WALK 13: MOORLAND WALK FROM THORNTON RUST

Start: Thornton Rust. Grid Ref: 972 889
Distance: 10½ miles (17km)
OS Maps: Outdoor Leisure 30 or Landranger 98
Walking Time: 5 hours

This fine moorland walk is mostly on unfrequented green lanes and bridleways, climbing gradually to an altitude of 1,770 feet (540m). It skirts Addlebrough, one of the dominant landmarks of the dale, visits Carpley Green and has panoramic views of Bishopdale and Wensleydale. Moorland birds and geology are of outstanding interest. There are no shops, pubs or other conveniences on the way – unless you make a short descent into Thoralby village – so take all you need and be prepared not to see anybody all day. There is limited parking in the village.

Thornton Rust has a spectacular position on a platform of the Hardraw limestone and, on a minor road, overlooks the dale in splendid fashion. It has an attractive wide street of stone cottages, houses and farms, some of which still have outside stone steps to a second floor. Nearby is the long, wooded Thornton Scar, and behind the village an area of springs, shakeholes and swallow holes.

Go up the lane opposite the village institute, cross a ford and continue up the green lane. At the ford West Beck washes the limestone clean to reveal a collection of fossil brachiopod shells deeply embedded in it. The lane zigzags up the hill and, at the end of it, the path turns left towards open country. Aim roughly for the slopes of Addlebrough, on its left side. This is Thornton Rust Moor, the home of curlew, lapwing, skylark, golden plover and meadow pipit. The skylark is one of our best-loved birds, and can keep up a continuous song for five minutes without a pause. It delivers its rippling melody while climbing vertically into the sky, hanging poised almost out of sight, and still continues as it comes down, finally dropping to the ground. To hear two or three of these songsters around you on a spring day is an unforgettable experience,

and their sheer vitality has aroused poets such as Shelley and Wordsworth to praise these 'blithe spirits' and 'pilgrims of the sky'. The golden plover! Is this not Wensleydale's own emblem? It takes over its breeding grounds from March to September, and hails visitors with its mournful 'tlee' call. The handsome summer plumage sparkles like pure gold when the sun shines, and the black breast and belly give it an aristocratic appearance. If disturbed while sitting on the eggs, the bird will feign a broken wing to lead you away from the nest.

After a wall, the path turns along a ridge with a small glaciated valley to the left, excavated in the softer shales between Addlebrough and the scarp of Stony Raise. Addlebrough (the 'brough' rhymes with rough) has an Iron Age fort on the top and a cairn, the possible burial place of the British chief, Authulf, who gave his name to the hill. On the far shelf of Stony Raise there are Iron Age fields and a large stone-covered burial cairn, in which a skeleton has been found. Legend has it that a giant came by carrying a heavy chest full of gold, calling:

'Spite of either God or man,
To Pendragon Castle thou shalt gang.'
The chest fell and sank into the ground,

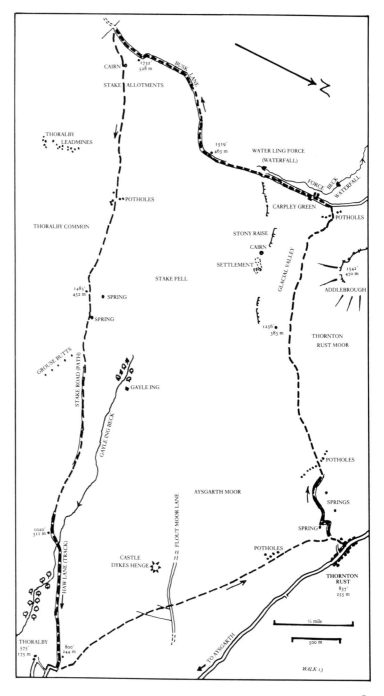

CAIRN • 1732'
          528 m

STAKE ALLOTMENTS

BUSK LANE

THORALBY
• LEADMINES

1519'
463 m

WATER LING FORCE
(WATERFALL)

FORCE BECK

WATERFALL

•POTHOLES

CARPLEY GREEN

POTHOLES

THORALBY COMMON

STONY RAISE

CAIRN

SETTLEMENT

GLACIAL VALLEY

1542'
470 m

STAKE FELL

ADDLEBROUGH

1483'
452 m   • SPRING

• SPRING

1256'
383 m

THORNTON
RUST MOOR

GROUSE BUTTS

STAKE ROAD (PATH)

• GAYLE ING

GAYLE ING BECK

POTHOLES

AYSGARTH MOOR

SPRINGS

SPRING

1020'
311 m

FLOUT MOOR LANE

POTHOLES

HAW LANE (TRACK)

CASTLE
DYKES HENGE

THORNTON
RUST
837'
255 m

½ mile

500 m

THORALBY
575'
175 m   800'
          244 m

TO AYSGARTH

WALK 13

83

and the stones covered it. A mortal will be able to find the treasure when a fairy appears as an ape or a hen, but the chest has to be removed in complete silence.

The way passes over the brow of the hill and drops down to Carpley Green. This is a fine old Pennine farm, isolated in its magnificent position at the foot of the stepped outline of Addlebrough and standing at almost 1,250 feet (380m) above sea level. From a few paces up the lane, there is a wonderful view looking back at the farm with its protective group of trees, the scar along the top of Addlebrough (the Underset limestone) and the green lane itself in the foreground. Swallows, wheatear and snipe live here. Swallows are commonly seen around farm buildings, where the same birds will return year after year, but the wheatear likes the open spaces where a few rocks or old walls provide it with a nest site. The snipe, with its long bill and attractively-patterned plumage, seldom allows close approach. It is most active in the morning and evening, but you may flush one as it calls out and flies away in a low zigzag. You may be lucky to hear it drumming, when its tail feathers vibrate to produce the characteristic sound as it

Snipe.

sideslips through the air. If you are close enough you can see the two outer tail feathers, separate from the tail itself, and it is these that make the throbbing sound 'vuvuvuvuvuvuvu'.

Just off the track to the right is Water Ling Force, where sandstone overlies shale and a pretty waterfall results, shrouded in mosses and rowans. Higher up, the path reaches the Underset limestone, and fossil corals, both colonial (macaroni-shaped) and simple (like an ice-cream cone), are visible in the rocks and in the walls. Busk Lane has a well-cobbled surface and, by an outcrop of limestone, mossy saxifrage grows well. Where the wall becomes broken, the stone is buff-coloured and the large brachiopod *Gigantoproductus* is present.

After the hairpin bend and just before the next gate, turn back on yourself, passing a cairn on your left and striking out east-north-east for the return route across Stake Allotments. The rock here is the Main limestone and there are one or two old leadmine shafts near the path with spring sandwort and mossy saxifrage, while common violets and wild thyme are dotted about. The path is not well worn and care is needed to find the way, but it is fairly straight, so carry on to a gate then through two large gateposts (railway sleepers) which stand out ahead, and aim roughly for Penhill in the distance. A signpost then indicates the path along a wall descending into a basin backed by limestone hills and heather-covered peat.

Go through a metal gate with its own sheep gate within it. In the broken wall are several fossil corals of the *Dibunophyllum* type. This simple coral is typical of the Underset limestone. In cross-section it is round and measures an inch or so (2 or 3cm) across. It has radiating partitions, known as septa, which look like the spokes of a wheel with an extra-strong partition

84

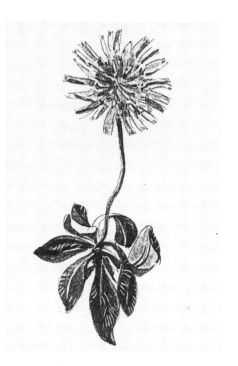

Mouse-eared hawkweed.

across the middle. There is a fresh spring of clear water nearby, and mossy saxifrage grows where the water goes under the wall.

The path still aims for Penhill as it continues along the top of a ridge. To the left is the remote cottage of Gayle Ing and a barn. This is a possible escape route, through the small gate in the wall, a stile by the barn and a footpath direct to Thornton Rust. Our route continues through a large metal gate along the crest of the ridge, where Ivy Scar comes into view on the left. Carperby, Preston-under-Scar and Bolton Castle are all visible across the dale. There are such amazing views on this walk! The quarry at Leyburn Shawl appears on the skyline and Penhill looms ever larger.

After passing through a blue metal gate, go down the green lane named Haw Lane, with new vistas into Bishopdale, and across to the village of West Burton. The lane is lined with mouse-eared hawkweed, lady's bedstraw, milkwort, tormentil and speedwell. Mouse-eared hawkweed, a short-stemmed, bright yellow flower, grows in short turf with a rosette of green leaves flat on the ground. It is distinguished by the streaks of crimson under the petals and the white underside of the leaves. Lady's bedstraw is a common species of old grassland, with its tiny yellow four-petalled flowers and whorls of narrow leaves. Flowering in July and August, it smells of new-mown hay.

At the corner of Haw Lane (which goes down the hill into Thoralby) turn sharp left uphill through the field. Unfortunately a detour into the village involves a drop in height of 250 feet (75m) and a stiff climb back, though this may not deter some. The route to Thornton Rust is straight but rises and falls over several ridges. At the top of the field, go diagonally to the far corner of the next, to cross the small stream of Haw Beck. Then keep the same direction to the 'invisible' stile ahead, and across to the next stile near Flout Moor Lane. Two more stiles bring you across the green lane, and the path continues alongside a wall to ford Gill Beck. The next bit entails skirting a newly-fenced field within a field, to continue in the same line. Some map reading may be necessary, though a distinct track eventually emerges and drops down the scar of the Simonstone limestone and back to Thornton Rust.

WALK 14: MILL GILL FROM ASKRIGG

Start: Askrigg. Grid Ref: 948 910
Distance: 3½ miles (5½ km)
OS Maps: Outdoor Leisure 30 or Landranger 98
Walking Time: 2½ hours

This short walk is full of interest and too good to hurry. It visits two of the finest waterfalls in the dale.
From Askrigg the route takes you to Mill Gill Force, passes through Helm, then up to Whitfield Gill to
see its own fine waterfall. There is a wealth of flowers and birdlife in the woods, and the geology is
outstanding. Children enjoy this walk, which includes some steep paths. The walk returns along Low
Straights Lane back to Askrigg.

Askrigg is recorded in the *Domesday Book*, and through the Middle Ages was on the edge of a hunting forest that occupied upper Wensleydale. Its position led to the growth of the village as a market town and commercial centre. Many of the three storey houses in the main street were built during the seventeenth and eighteenth centuries, when the town was booming. In 1795 the new turnpike road bypassed Askrigg, and Hawes developed as the main market centre in its place. However, Askrigg has not lost the character of a small market town and is popular with visitors. It has some good eating places.

From the market cross, start off along West End on the north side of the church. You will see comfrey growing along the lane. This is a tall plant with hairy leaves, and flowers in a variety of shades. It has long been used for setting bones, when the grated or crushed roots were placed round the broken limb where it hardened like plaster of Paris. At the end of the lane, cross a flowery meadow to the former saw mill, now used as a residential youth centre. The beck here runs in a natural rock bed of the Gayle limestone, and overhead is an unusual galvanised iron aqueduct which carried water over the path to the water wheel, still in position inside the building.

After crossing the bridge, the path continues up the left side of the beck and into the wood. In spring and early summer there is a profusion of flowers and birds in this small beech and sycamore wood, and it is worth taking time to look around you. Among the more obvious wild flowers are bluebells, wild garlic, herb robert, wood sanicle, wood avens, water avens and greater stitchwort. The bluebell is a very British flower as it does not grow beyond the near part of the Continent. It grows deep in the ground from a small bulb which contains a sticky juice once used as glue in the making of arrows. Wood sanicle has several small tight flower clusters in its white flower-head. It has been regarded as having the power to cure all kinds of ailments. Its hooked seeds stick easily to clothing or to an animal's fur, thus spreading them far and wide. The wood is incredibly luxuriant with mosses, liverworts and ferns, which grow strongly around seepages and within reach of the spray from the waterfall.

Among the birds, wood warbler, nuthatch, tree creeper, willow warbler, long-tailed tit, chaffinch and wren are all to be heard or seen. The wood warbler lives only in mature woods like this where there is a thick canopy of leaves and where it feeds on

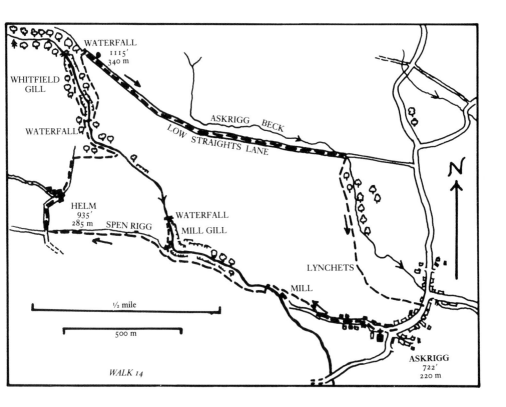

the insect life. You may hear its harsh trill which carries through the chorus of bird-song. The nuthatch is with us all year, and is the only bird you may see which climbs down trees head first. It builds its nest in a hole in a tree but will also use a nest box. And near the falls you will see grey wagtail, dipper and jackdaws. The grey wagtail is very much at home by a rushing stream and is often seen in the company of dippers. In spite of its name it is a very colourful bird, with its bright yellow underparts, black throat and tail, and blue-grey back.

Follow the 'Mill Gill Only' sign to reach the falls. This is the beginning of a classic exposure of Yoredale rocks. The whole of Mill Gill and Whitfield Gill form a very fine, almost continuous succession of the Yoredale strata. At Mill Gill Force the whitish rock at the top is Hardraw limestone, halfway down you can make out the darker sandstone, and in the stream bed, black shales outcrop. The bottom of the waterfall has been hollowed out in the softer shales by the force of the falling water to form a plunge pool.

Return to the path up the side of the wood, and at the top corner take the footpath signed 'Helm ½ mile' through the fields known as Spen Rigg. There are wonderful views from here across the dale to Bainbridge and into Raydale. At the walled lane, turn right and right again in front of the group of houses which make up Helm. This former hamlet lies on the old pack-horse route of Lady Anne Clifford's Way, which runs from Askrigg through to Hardraw and Hell Gill and on to Kirkby

87

Mill Gill Force

Stephen. Helm was for some years the home of Geoffrey Wright, author and authority on the Dales, and in his book *Roads and Trackways of the Yorkshire Dales* he describes the retinue that accompanied Lady Anne in the 1660s. As High Sheriff of Westmorland she travelled like royalty and, having stayed with her cousin Thomas Metcalfe at Nappa Hall, passed this way with a train of some 300 people in coaches, on horseback and driving horse wagons as they made their way from one castle to the next. No wonder the local people still talked centuries later of 'Lady Anne's road'.

From Helm, the path climbs up through a field and turns right to arrive at the gill once again. In the beck, just above this point, there are some beds of limestone which form a small waterfall with shale beneath and a plunge pool. Below the shale

Wood cranesbill.

and visible in the bank of the stream is an eight inch (20cm) thick coal seam and a 'seat earth'. The coal is the compacted remains of rain forest peat of 335 million years ago, and the seat earth is the fossil soil in which the the trees grew. Higher up, a thick sandstone outcrops on the side of the gill and forms another small waterfall just below the footbridge.

Instead of going directly down to the footbridge, keep high up on the left side of the ravine, following the sign to Whitfield Force. Spotted orchids grow on the edge of the wood, with yellow pimpernel, bluebell, wood sorrel, wood speedwell, woodruff and wood cranesbill. The common spotted orchid can be a variety of shades from white to deep pink, with a pointed flower spike, the leaves having elongated blotches. Yellow pimpernel has pointed pairs of leaves and bright yellow flowers of five petals, and is typical of damp woods. Woodruff, *Galium odoratum*, is of the bedstraw family and its pure white flowers prefer the calcareous soils of old beech woods. The leaves, like meadow grasses, contain a chemical which when dried smells of new-mown hay, and the plant spreads by creeping underground stems.

The path gradually descends into the gorge, formed here by the Simonstone limestone, and eventually you will see the impressive waterfall of Whitfield Force. At the top of the fall is a thin sandstone, below which are thick shales. The shales at the foot of the falls contain fragments of fossil corals and brachiopods. Some of the shell ornament is nicely preserved in the shale.

Return along the same route to the footbridge. Climb up the east side of the gill to emerge at the top of Low Straights Lane. Again there are wonderful views from this elevated track. Just before the ford, where Askrigg Beck crosses the lane, turn right across the fields and down the hill back to Askrigg.

WALK 15: SEMERWATER, COUNTERSETT AND MARSETT

Start:	Bainbridge. Grid Ref: 934 902
Distance:	9 miles (15½ km)
OS Maps:	Outdoor Leisure 30 or Landranger 98
Walking Time:	5 hours

This lovely, hilly walk visits the three small villages of Countersett, Marsett and Stalling Busk, the only natural lake in Wensleydale and a short stretch of the Roman road. There are some steep paths, breathtaking views and a great variety of interest along the way. There is parking alongside the green in Bainbridge.

Bainbridge is the most picturesque of Wensleydale's villages, with most of its eighteenth and nineteenth century houses facing the large green. Originally the village grew as a base for foresters, and the ancient custom of blowing a horn each evening through the winter is still carried on. The sound of the horn was to guide late travellers in the forest to a promise of food and shelter. So listen for its deep notes around nine o'clock in the evening between the 28th September and Shrove Tuesday. During the summer months the horn is hung in the Rose and Crown. Low Mill has been restored to working order and its great waterwheel turns once again for the interested visitor.

Go to the top end of the green, which is the oldest part of the village, and notice a cottage which was formerly the Old Dame School where reading, writing and arithmetic cost 2d per pupil per week.

Cross over the bridge from which you can see the River Bain cascading over steps in the Gayle limestone, pass a garage and take the footpath on the right labelled 'Semerwater 2'. The river, said to be the shortest in England at only two and a half miles (4km) long, runs over the Great Scar limestone in the bottom of a deep gorge. On the far side is a fine display of beeches, providing a colourful scene in the autumn.

Climb up alongside the wall and curve uphill to reach the brow of Bracken Hill, a large drumlin. From the top, keep straight on, parallel to the river valley. The path continues over two or three stiles down towards the riverbank. The next part of the river is in total contrast to the lower part. It is slow-moving over a flat area, with water plants lining its route. In fact, the River Bain turns the textbook on its head. This river starts with a very gentle gradient, speeds up in the gorge over stones and boulders, cuts through solid rock and finally tumbles over waterfalls at its lower end into Bainbridge – just the opposite of any normal river! This is because at its upper end it is blocked by glacial drift which increases the gradient lower down.

The water plants below Semerwater Bridge are a fascinating collection. The large leathery leaves of the yellow water lily and its bright yellow flowers add dignity to the picturesque scene, where thatching reeds and stately grasses grow tall. Great burnet, marsh ragwort, devilsbit scabious and meadowsweet line the banks in summer, and, in the slow-moving water, amphibious bistort sends up its pink flowery spikes. This is a remarkable plant with two forms, a land plant with hairy leaves and shorter stems, and the more showy aquatic form with hairless floating leaves and longer stalks.

Arrival at the triple-arched Semerwater

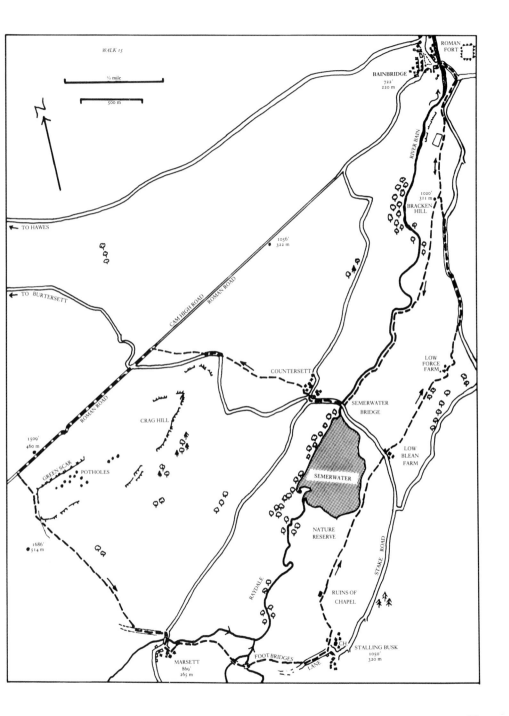

WALK 15

¼ mile

500 m

TO HAWES

TO BURTERSETT

N

CAM HIGH ROAD   ROMAN ROAD

ROMAN ROAD

GREEN SCAR

POTHOLES

CRAG HILL

1509'
460 m

1686'
514 m

1056'
322 m

COUNTERSETT

SEMERWATER
BRIDGE

SEMERWATER

NATURE
RESERVE

RAYDALE

STAKE ROAD

RUINS OF
CHAPEL

FOOT BRIDGES   LANE

MARSETT
869'
265 m

CH   STALLING BUSK
1050'
320 m

BAINBRIDGE
722'
220 m

RIVER BAIN

1020'
311 m
BRACKEN
HILL

LOW
FORCE
FARM

LOW
BLEAN
FARM

ROMAN
FORT

Bainbridge.

Bridge brings you to a view of Semerwater itself. The lake is a relic of the Ice Age, having been dammed by morainic material at its lower end. It was formerly several times bigger and stretched far up the dale. A large erratic block of limestone, stranded by glacial ice and known as the Carlow Stone, is prominent near the road. The area is now a Site of Special Scientific Interest. In spite of its use for leisure activities such as fishing, boating, wind-surfing and swimming, the lake attracts some interesting birdlife. It shouldn't be difficult to spot the long neck and pointed bill of the great crested grebe. In the breeding season, the grebes acquire chest-nut frills on the side of the face and much brighter plumage than in the winter.

Courtship displays are elaborate cere-monies of neck-stretching and head-shaking, and are commonly seen. Other birds present on the lake include coot, mallard, tufted duck and heron. In winter a flock of whooper swans visit the lake.

Semerwater has its own legend of a sunken city, immortalised in *The Ballad of Semerwater* by Sir William Watson. The story is of a beggar rejected by all the selfish villagers except one old couple who took him in, and how in turn he caused the lake to swallow the village 'save this little house'. There is evidence of a lake dwelling built on stilts, which could date back to the Neolithic period. A recent and more tan-gible tradition is that of the Semerwater Service, started in 1956. (Both are described by Julia Smith in her book *Fairs, Feasts and Frolics*.) On August Bank Holiday Sunday, the Vicar of Askrigg and Stalling Busk gives an open-air service from a boat on the lake to a large congregation on the shore, with Hawes Brass Band to accompany the hymns.

From the bridge, turn up the road to Countersett. The short climb gives a good view of the lake, the river flowing into it, and to the left, the sharp edge of Addlebrough. Countersett is a haphazard collection of old houses in a hollow. The hall was the home of Richard Robinson, the first Quaker in Wensleydale, and George Fox stayed here in 1677. The building retains a fine porch, carved oak panels and stone-mullioned windows. The Quaker meeting house dates from 1710 and is still in use today.

At the top of the village, take the path signed 'Hawes End' through an iron gate up the fields, past two barns to a stile at the top, then across and up to the road. From the steep ascent there are magnificent views of Semerwater and Addlebrough. You are now on the brow of the hill known as Hawes End. To the left is the steep end of Crag Hill, capped by the Underset limestone. Turn right along the road for a new view to Wether Fell, Yoreburgh and upper Wensleydale. After a hundred yards or so, go through the stile, down across rough pasture to a gated stile and onto the Roman road.

The route continues for a mile (1½ km) up this ancient highway. This is one of the best-preserved Roman roads in the Dales and runs from Ingleton to the fort at Bainbridge. The road is absolutely straight over this stretch, except for a small waver at New Bridge where the crossing of a small gulley has been reconstructed. The sound of marching legionaries died away long ago, and in more recent centuries this was an important drove road which throbbed with

the tramp of thousands of sheep and cattle on their way south. In the 1990s there is little to disturb the creamy flowers of mossy saxifrage or the delicate blue harebells that nod in the summer sunshine.

About 550 yards (500m) above New Bridge (the kink in the road), turn left through the stile signed 'Marsett'. The stile has a broad arrow on the step with a brass stud. This is one of the older type of bench marks denoting height above sea level, here being approximately 1,500 feet (460m). Climb up to the 'pass' and over to a lovely view of Raydale, with Buckden Pike at the top end. There is a small quarry on the right with a limekiln below it, and a view of the scar of Underset limestone along the top of Crag Hill.

The right of way goes straight down the hill to the left of the wall to join the lane leading into Marsett. This quiet hamlet seems to be from another age, its small cluster of sombre farmhouses standing before a broad common. Beyond it, a mile or so higher up the dale, the metalled road comes to an end. It was near this point that the Raydale borehole was made, which reached the Wensleydale granite in June 1973, 1,624 feet (495m) below the surface. Along the road between Marsett and Countersett lies Carr End, the house where Dr John Fothergill, the famous Quaker, was born in 1712. Besides being a great botanist and doctor (he was the first to diagnose diphtheria), he was the founder of Ackworth School near Pontefract, a boarding school which pioneered education on an equal basis for boys and girls.

Continue alongside Marsett Beck, then along a walled lane to a footbridge over Raydale Beck to another footbridge over Cragdale Water. Go through the fields and up to Busk Lane to the village of Stalling Busk. Here on the hillside at over 1,000 feet (320m) above sea level are the farms, barns, cottages, village hall (formerly the school) and St Matthews Parish Church of Stalling Busk. The church, which has a resemblance to a Swiss chalet, was built in 1909.

Go left through the village and turn left at the sign for the ruined church. This was formerly the church for the village and the graveyard is still used. Built in 1722, it replaced an earlier one on the same site. It was a small building, but the ruins are attractive with the stone arches still in position looking onto Semerwater below.

A little further on you pass through the margin of Semerwater nature reserve managed by the Yorkshire Wildlife Trust. It is a marshy area, once the bed of a larger lake, but now a haven for several interesting plants. Along the shore grow clumps of bulrushes, thatching reeds, yellow water lilies, bogbean, marsh cinquefoil and bottle sedge, and this is a good place to view the birds which make use of the vegetation cover.

At the road, go through the farmyard of Low Blean farm and flowery fields to the next farm, Low Force. Cross the farm track to the ladder stile. Beyond the farm, follow the cart track up to the road. Then, after two-thirds of a mile (1km) along the road, turn left over a ladder stile and up to the far left corner of the field beyond the brow of the hill. Join the footpath on which this walk started out. On the way down into Bainbridge there are magnificent views of Wensleydale and of the remains of the Roman fort perched on its drumlin hilltop. The fort on Brough Hill was named Virosidum and was the largest in the Dales. It was occupied for over 300 years from AD 80 until the withdrawal in AD 395. Agricola stationed 500 Roman soldiers here when it was first built, and local British attacked it on more than one occasion. Today there are grassy mounds and ridges left as reminders.

WALK 16: BAINBRIDGE, SKELLGILL, ASKRIGG AND WORTON

Start: Bainbridge. Grid Ref: 934 902
Distance: 8½ miles (13½ km)
OS Maps: Outdoor Leisure 30 or Landranger 98
Walking Time: 4½ hours

A figure of eight, this walk may be taken one half at a time or in its entirety. The Skellgill part is a quiet rural stroll and full of interest for its birds and plants. The slightly shorter loop goes through the charming village of Askrigg and the hamlet of Worton, along Worton Scar and back to Bainbridge.

The many stone houses which overlook an exceptionally large green makes Bainbridge a very attractive village. At the north end of the town stands the fine old coaching inn, the Rose and Crown – the arms of Yorkshire – where the forest horn is hung in summer. The building dates from the fifteenth century but was rebuilt in Victorian times. On the east side of the green is Low Mill, the waterwheel and working parts of which have been restored into motion and are open to the public. Power is from the River Bain, England's shortest river. Brough Hill overlooks the village on the east side and the Roman soldiers who built the fort here must have had a commanding view from the top.

Begin by passing between the inn and the Quaker meeting house, built in 1836 and still in use, along the Askrigg road to the River Ure. On the right just before the bridge is Yorebridge House, formerly the old grammar school (c1840) with the headmaster's house next to it; both are now National Park offices. Yore Bridge has three segmented arches and may date from about the 1790s, replacing an earlier one.

Cross the bridge, go through the stile on the left of the road and cross the old railway (to the left of the bridge). The path passes to the right of Yorecotts Farm to regain the road. Turn left along the road for 110 yards (100m) then off to the right, signposted

'Skell Gill '. The path leads you over the shoulder of a drumlin. From here you can see Coleby Hall, built in 1655, an E-shaped Tudor manor house with rooms over the porch, a spiral staircase and an impressive stone doorway.

Go down and through a stile between two gates and up to a gap in the wall on the crest of the hill. The path continues to the little hamlet of Skellgill. The beck runs into a miniature gorge, then through Grange Gill Wood and here, among the woodland birds, you may see the green woodpecker. This is the largest and most colourful of the woodpeckers, being mainly a dull green with a red crown and yellow rump. It is a tree-climber and borer of holes, but will feed as much on the ground as on tree trunks, using a long, sticky tongue as it probes for ants, larvae or seeds.

Skellgill consists of a hump-backed packhorse bridge, a working farm and two or three cottages, but it was once a livelier place. The track from Scargill Mine, an old, rich leadmine which had its own smeltmill, comes down from the fells through here, and the old road of Lady Anne Clifford's renown passes through, on its way from Askrigg to Hardraw.

Turn left along the lane past two cottages, and left again before the ford. There is a glimpse of Penhill to remind you where you are, but this is such a lovely spot,

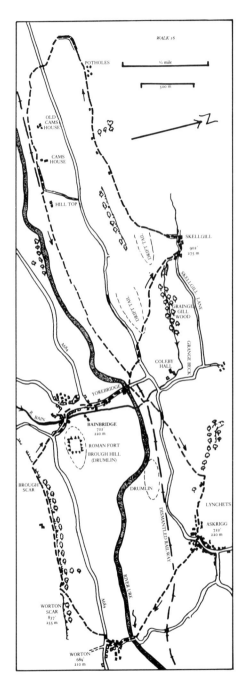

you might imagine you were in some other newly-discovered dale. The fantasy is short-lived, however, as the track curves sharply to the left, you descend to a wall and are truly in Wensleydale again. Pass a line of four farms, some of which are fine buildings with arched windows, all of them facing the south, thereby benefitting most from the sunshine. Windows are rare on north-facing walls and few were built on west walls in the path of the westerly winds.

Join a walled green lane which curves to the left. From the gate at the end of the lane, keep curving left and descend to the road. The return route crosses the road, passes through some outcrops of limestone, and keeps to the right of Old Camshouse to join a narrow lane. In summer the grass verges are full of flowers and, on the left, a grand avenue of lime trees lead to Camshouse. The common lime is a cross between small-leaved and broad-leaved limes, and is distinguished by its many sprouts and bosses on the trunk. It has clusters of six or seven flowers which produce rounded fruits. The best of flower tea can be made from the dried flowers. On the right is the old railway and, beyond that, the river with a stepping stone crossing.

Where the lane turns sharply away, the walk continues along the former railway track. This section of line from Leyburn to Hawes was opened in 1878. It was closed in 1964, but there is talk of opening it up once again in the future.

To start the second loop of the figure of eight, cross the road at Yore Bridge, go through the field on a flagstone way, 'under' the railway and over the delightful, stone hump-backed bridge, complete with iron handrail, to the hamlet of Grange. Fors Abbey, founded in 1145, was the first monastery to be built in Wensleydale. It was probably of timber and its site is where the quiet hamlet of Grange stands today. The monks worked hard to establish their

Askrigg.

farm here, but after eleven years a better place was found at Jervaulx, where they moved in 1156. Little evidence remains today but when construction of the railway was in progress, navvies unearthed human skeletons and, nearby, lengths of lead waterpipe leading to the site of Fors Abbey. A piece of the lead pipe is now in the museum at Hawes. The abbey was kept as a grange and chantry chapel until the dis-solution. The grange was a means of man-aging the large Jervaulx estate and included a working farm. It was led by a priest-monk, aided by lay brothers, with local people carrying out work on the farm. The grange may have been rebuilt in stone as a few old carved stones are to be seen, for example in a barn at Grange and in Worton Hall.

The path comes out onto the road to the right of the village of Grange and, eighty yards (73m) further on, strikes across the fields to the footbridge over Mill Gill. Up from the road the hillside is a drift tail, one of a pair of these glacial mounds which have diverted the waters of Mill Gill Beck eastwards to create the waterfalls of Mill Gill. Looking to the right there is the perfect shape of a drumlin, steep on the upstream side with Addlebrough behind it.

As you go up the over the rise and look down to the cottages and former saw mill on Mill Gill, there is a remarkable view of lynchets, the ancient strip fields which swoop down towards Askrigg. Behind the village is a rounded glacial hill, another drumlin, and in the distance is Ivy Scar in the Underset limestone. The flat valley floor is the bed of a former glacial lake.

Go over the footbridge and past the mill – where the waterwheel is still in position – through a field of lynchets, an amazing flowery meadow in June, and along the lane

Worton Hall.

into Askrigg. Quite different from Bainbridge, yet just as attractive, this charming old village squeezes between small glacial hills, and its crowded buildings face each other across the steep, winding street.

Take the road opposite the market cross through the cottages and, shunning the tempting walled lane on the left, go straight down through a field and across the old railway. The route is along the flagged path, well-built stiles and over Worton Bridge to the hamlet of Worton (the name rhymes with Burton). There are some interesting old houses here including, on the right, Worton Hall, built in 1600, one of the oldest domestic buildings in the dale. Its low roof and stone-mullioned windows make it one of the most charming of old Dales farmhouses. Near the corner with the main road, opposite the telephone box, is a house inscribed: '1729, Michael Smith, Mechanick, But He that built all things is God'. In 1757 there was a bread riot in Worton. Corn was delivered to the village for gentlemen in the upper dale and a riotous mob stole most of it. The mob also

went round demanding money from people in Bainbridge and Askrigg. Several offenders ended up in Richmond Jail.

Turn right at the main road, and, after a few paces, go left through a gate, diagonally up to the top of the field and onto Worton Scar. This narrow stretch of woodland which clings to the scar of Hardraw limestone is a mile (1,600m) long, and there is another length towards Thornton Rust. It has many woodland flowers such as the primrose, bluebell, wood cranesbill, early purple orchid, and goldilocks. The last one is a member of the buttercup family. The distorted, golden-yellow flower appears to have only two or three petals. The shy roe deer finds a refuge in the wood, so don't be surprised to catch sight of one. They are not much bigger than a large dog, have very short tails and when alarmed they fluff out the pale hairs of the rump like a large powder puff.

Towards the end of the scar there is a good view of the Roman fort on the drumlin of Brough hill, and the path descends to the road which leads back into Bainbridge.

98

WALK 17: BURTERSETT AND WETHER FELL

Start: Burtersett. Grid Ref: 890 893
Distance: 6 miles (10 km)
OS Maps: Outdoor Leisure 30 or Landranger 98
Walking Time: 3 hours

Starting from the village of Burtersett, just over a mile (2km) from Hawes, this scenic walk takes you first on a barn trail towards Gayle, then turns up onto Wether Fell, almost a 1,000 foot (300m) climb. Beyond the flint quarry there are outstanding views into Sleddale and the upper part of Wensleydale. After visiting the cairn at the top, the route joins the Roman road for a short distance before an easy descent on a bridleway to end the walk. There is limited parking at the top end of the village.

Burtersett is a rather special village. It even looks different from other Dales villages. However, it does have the same origin as Appersett, Gayle and Sedbusk, that of a summer farm or shieling, from the Norse word *saetr*. There are one or two older buildings, some with dated lintels over the door, but the tall houses were built in the 1880s for the quarrymen. They are architect-designed and constructed of stone from the new quarries. The quarries are in fact mines, tunnelled some distance into the hillside, mainly for the production of roofing stone. The flagstone lies just below the Middle limestone, but of the four metre thick sandstone bed, only one and a half metres is quality stone. The reason why this sandstone makes good roofing material is because embedded in it are tiny flakes of mica which lie flat with the bedding and enable the rock to be split easily. Three mine entrances and their spoil heaps are situated on the hillside above High Lane. Many of the tunnels show signs of collapse and are dangerous to enter. David Hall describes the industry in his little book *Burtersett Quarries, a Wensleydale Mining Community*.

Start at the top end of the village to the right along the narrow, walled Shaws Lane. Between Burtersett and Gayle there is the unusual situation of a chain of seventeen field barns, fascinating to those interested in Dales stone buildings and vernacular architecture. Of the late eighteenth century, they are generally very well built, using good-quality stone with lines of 'throughs' which jut out at regular intervals on the outside walls. The barns all look similar, but in detail no two of them are alike. Those with a lean-to or 'offshut' may have it built on the side, part of a side or at the end of the building. One very large barn has four portals for loading hay into the loft, and the position and number of doors varies with each one. Swallows and swifts find the barns useful nesting sites in the summer, and the unmown patches around them contain colourful foxglove, knapweed, harebell, meadow cranesbill and ragwort.

At the tenth barn, follow the finger post indicating Gayle to the left and, after the next ladder stile, turn left through a red metal gate by barn number eleven. Go up the middle of the field to a squeezer stile in the wall, from which you get a view of the next six barns towards Gayle. Go up the once-wooded hillside to the third squeezer stile by a little waterfall and a small group of rowans, alder and ash, then to more waterfalls a bit higher up. The beck is called Blackburn Sike and the sandstone here is the same as that quarried in the

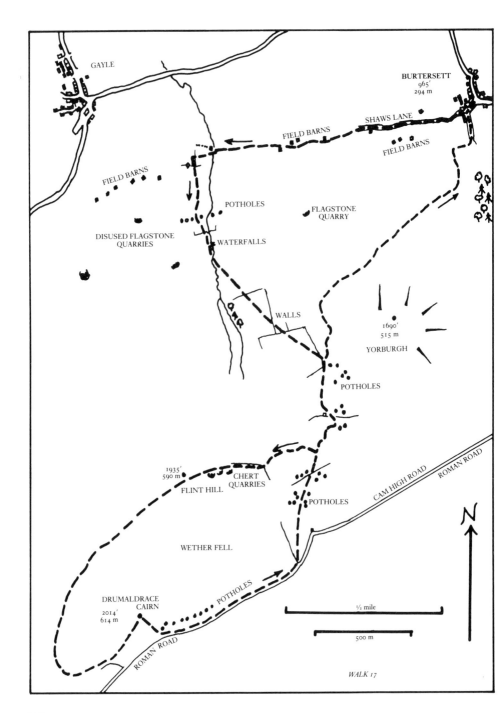

GAYLE

BURTERSETT
965'
294 m

SHAWS LANE

FIELD BARNS

FIELD BARNS

FIELD BARNS

POTHOLES

FLAGSTONE
QUARRY

DISUSED FLAGSTONE
QUARRIES

WATERFALLS

WALLS

1690'
515 m

YORBURGH

POTHOLES

1935'
590 m

CHERT
QUARRIES

FLINT HILL

CAM HIGH ROAD

ROMAN ROAD

POTHOLES

WETHER FELL

DRUMALDRACE
CAIRN
2014'
614 m

POTHOLES

ROMAN ROAD

½ mile

500 m

N

WALK 17

The Drumaldrace cairn on Wether Fell, and Addlebrough in the distance.

Burtersett mines. Cross the stream and aim for the middle of the top of the pasture, then the top left corner of the next two pastures to join the bridleway from Burtersett. At this point the walls and flora indicate a limestone (the Underset limestone).

The winding, well-graded quarry track leads up to a gate at the top of the hill at the end of Wether Fell. From here, follow the wall on the right and you soon come to Flint Hill quarry, with a cairn made of chert. The chert bed is an unusual rock, consisting of large lumps of this flinty stone embedded in limestone. On weathered blocks the brownish limestone contrasts with the grey chert. Or you can tell the difference by using a penknife as limestone scratches and chert doesn't. It is extremely hard and was quarried for use in the ceramic industry and for grinding. Like flint in composition, it is made up of very finely crystalline silica. Although early prehistoric man used chert for such things as hand axes and scrapers, flint was much superior as it was easier to work, though of course it had to be brought into the area from east Yorkshire where it occurs in the chalk. Below the chert is the

Main limestone, which forms the edge of the fell and which has many shakeholes eroded into it. Peat covers most of the top of the fell.

The buzzard frequents the moors, soaring and circling, eagle-like and unhurried, on broad, rigid wings. It is the most common of the large birds of prey and, although a brown bird, shows a variety of shades and patterns among individuals. If mobbed by crows or seagulls, the buzzard will continue flying on to outdistance them, but occasionally will turn to face them with its talons.

The path follows round the north-west edge of the fell, with lovely views of Sleddale and across to Dodd Fell, eventually meeting the Roman road. Just before reaching this green lane, a short diversion up the slope leads you to the summit. The top fifty feet (15m) of Wether Fell are capped with millstone grit of which the cairn, known as Drumaldrace, is built. This point is 2,015 feet (614m) above sea level and on a clear day there is an extensive view. The scarp edge of Wild Boar Fell and the peaks of High Seat and Great Shunner Fell are the three highest points to the

Semerwater and Addlebrough.

north-west. To the east, Semerwater is visible.

Take the shortest way down from the cairn to join the wide track of the Roman road, some of which is on limestone bedrock. The Romans built the road to link Ingleton and Bainbridge with connections from Ribchester and Lancaster. At the point where the road is walled on both sides, go through the first gate on the left, and the bridleway strikes midway between the Roman road and the wall on the left, bisecting the angle.

Go through the gap in a wall to rejoin the route up for a short distance. The shoulder of Yorburgh with its scar of the Underset limestone lies ahead and, further down the path, there is a good view into Wensleydale. You can pick out the drumlins on the valley floor with their textbook shape, steep on the upstream side and gentle on the down; the best one has a group of sycamores on the top. To the left is Hawes, its church and the meandering River Ure nearby. On the far side of the dale you can make out the line of the old railway with trees dotted along it. The view of Burtersett just below shows the compact nature of the village, to which the path leads and where the walk ends.

WALK 18: HARDRAW FORCE AND STAGS FELL FROM HAWES

Start: Hawes. Grid Ref: 873 898
Distance: 8 miles (13km)
OS Maps: Outdoor Leisure 30 and Pathfinder 608, or Landranger 98
Walking Time: 4 hours

A start from Hawes gives the advantage of a riverside walk before a visit to the famous Hardraw Force. The route continues up to Stags Fell quarries, up the Buttertubs road for a short way, then turns onto the wide open fell and returns through Sedbusk. This is a pleasant walk with a total climb of nearly 1,000 feet (300m) from the River Ure to the shoulder of Stags Fell. Of particular interest are the flagstone quarries, the views, and the river and moorland birds.

The small market town of Hawes, still with its cobbled street, is the main tourist centre for Wensleydale. It received its market charter in 1700 and grew in importance after the turnpike road to Lancaster was opened in 1795. There are many hotels, restaurants, guest houses, camp sites and a youth hostel. This is the halfway stage of the Pennine Way, which passes through on its way to the Scottish border. The National Park visitor centre and the Dales Countryside Museum occupy the old railway buildings, with a large car park. The museum, founded by the historians Marie Hartley and Joan Ingilby, is outstanding for its collection of items reflecting a great range of past activities in the dale and should not be missed. Nearby is the ropeworks, where one old craft is still carried on. The cheese factory, founded by Kit Calvert, takes milk from some ninety farms, and 'baby Wensleydales' are popular with visitors. Hawes is the market centre for all the villages and farms of the upper dale, has a good variety of shops, a very large auction mart for sheep and cattle, and on Tuesdays an open-air market.

Starting near the upper end of Hawes, turn off the main street to the right opposite the 'chippie', finding a way round the ironmongers to the path that takes you under the line of the old railway and straight down to the riverbank. Walk downstream and follow the raised levée. Here on the floodplain of the River Ure is a fine place for some birdwatching. In the late spring there is much activity, as sand martins and swallows dive to and fro over the river, all three wagtails frequent the river meadows, and redshank and snipe announce their presence. The brightly-coloured yellow wagtail is a summer visitor and is at home by watery meadows or marshy land. The familiar redshank is a restless bird and will be the first to warn the other birds of your presence. You may see it dangling its red legs as it hovers and scolds a potential predator, its rump and wing bars showing white. Snipe also like poorly-drained wetlands. They are so well camouflaged that you rarely see them until they are flushed out, when they shoot up with a loud call. On a summer evening the males may be heard drumming as they slide through the air to vibrate their outer tail feathers.

The way is over Gayle Beck by the footbridge and the stile onto the road and over the elegant, double-arched Haylands Bridge. Take the first path to the left through a double gate and across a football field, with a tree-covered, sandstone and limestone scar to the right. Cross the step stile to join the Pennine Way and a

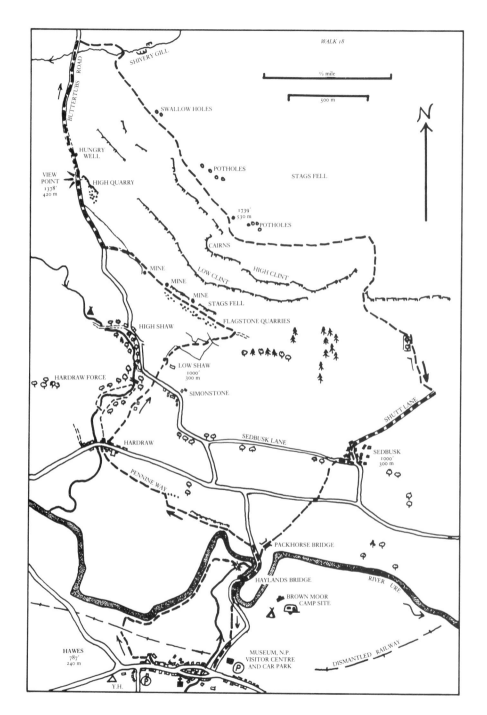

½ mile

500 m

N

SHIVERY GILL

BUTTERTUBS ROAD

SWALLOW HOLES

HUNGRY
WELL

VIEW
POINT
1378'
420 m

HIGH QUARRY

POTHOLES

STAGS FELL

1739'
530 m

POTHOLES

CAIRNS

MINE

LOW CLINT

HIGH CLINT

MINE

MINE

STAGS FELL

FLAGSTONE QUARRIES

HIGH SHAW

HARDRAW FORCE

LOW SHAW
1000'
300 m

SIMONSTONE

HARDRAW

SEDBUSK LANE

SHUTT LANE

SEDBUSK
1000'
300 m

PENNINE WAY

PACKHORSE BRIDGE

HAYLANDS BRIDGE

RIVER URE

BROWN MOOR
CAMP SITE

HAWES
787'
240 m

MUSEUM, N.P.
VISITOR CENTRE
AND CAR PARK

DISMANTLED RAILWAY

Y.H.

Hardraw Force in winter.

flagstone path to Hardraw. These paved ways are reminders that the quarrymen walked to and from work along here. Farmers complained that meadow grass was being trampled, so quarry owners provided the flags and the quarrymen layed them.

The little village of Hardraw is used to having many vistors, as its waterfall has been a tourist attraction for 200 years and has seen many visiting celebrities. It was a cold winter's day in 1799 when Wordsworth came, and he and his sister Dorothy stood behind the falls with icicles hanging from the rocks above, 'lofty and magnificent'. The great landscape painter Turner did a painting of the falls, from which he made a well-known engraving. In 1899 a cloudburst on Shunner Fell brought terrible floods to the village, washing away several gravestones and flooding the inn and nearby cottages. The water was so deep that in the Green Dragon Inn a large table floated in six feet (1.8m) of water.

To reach the falls, go through the Green Dragon, where a small charge is made. In

Dodd Fell, Ten End and Ingleborough: the view across Wensleydale from Stags Fell.

the spring the banks of the gorge as you approach the grand spectacle are clothed with red campion, primroses, forget-me-nots and St John's-wort, while high above, slender trees grace the edge of the cliff. The ninety foot (27m) drop of falling water into the natural rock bowl is impressive. It is possible to walk behind the falls and see the water racing down in front of you. Shales occur in the stream bed and to about a third of the way up the falls, then come sandstone and Hardraw limestone at the top, a complete cycle of Yoredale strata. The combination of soft shale below and hard limestone on top is the classic situation for the formation of a waterfall, the same as Niagara Falls. In 1739 and 1881, Hardraw Force froze into a pillar of ice, and about the turn of the century the lip of the falls collapsed and was rebuilt to restore its former appearance. The amphitheatre has such good acoustics that the annual brass band contest, begun in the 1880s, has been revived and is held here on the last Sunday in August.

A few years ago a Bradford school party, who were studying the geology of the Dales, found a piece of flagstone at Hardraw with fossil footprints on it. These turned out to be the tracks of an armoured, flesh-eating amphibian called *Megapezia*. The hind footprint measures two inches (5cm) long and has four 'toes'. They are the same as some found in Nova Scotia, Canada, reflecting the fact that the North American and European continents were still joined together at that time about 335,000,000 years ago (the Lower Carboniferous period). The footprints are the oldest tracks of a four-legged animal yet found in Britain and are now with the Natural History Museum in London.

Return to the Green Dragon, take the path to the right of the pub signed 'Simonstone Hall', up through the fields, past West House and left along the double track to the road at Simonstone. Simonstone Hall consists of a restaurant and holiday accommodation. Cross the road and up the farm track, round the right side of the barn at Low Shaw Farm to a six-barred wooden gate, and straight on up the field with the wall on your left to a ladder stile. Then go diagonally to the right to a stile at the highest point of the field. Continue in the same direction up through the bracken, between two spoil heaps of flagstone, onto the trail through the Stags Fell quarries. After the steep climb the path is now level, as it makes its way to the left through an

area once a hive of activity. Quarrymen toiled here in damp and dark conditions to get the valuable roofing stone. As at Burtersett, the stone was mined by tunnels into the hillside, and you will see two or three of the mine entrances along the way. There is a wonderful view from here across and up the dale.

Go through the gate and along the track to reach the Buttertubs road; then walk up to the viewpoint near the cattle grid. There is a magnificent view from here. Immediately below is Fossdale, a quiet little valley whose beck passes over Hardraw Force. Up the dale the row of hills include Dodd Fell, Widdale Fell and Baugh Fell.

From the cattle grid, continue along the unfenced road, which has posts to mark its edge during winter blizzards, to the brow of the hill. Just after crossing Shivery Gill, take the path to the right signposted 'Bridleway to Sedbusk'. Climb up onto the edge of Stags Fell, where the track turns right across Shivery Gill. The highest part of Stags Fell is Lovely Seat, and the old name of Abbotside Common dates from the time the land belonged to Jervaulx. The upper part of Shivery Gill is called Sod Hole Gill, and the watercourse is full of blocks of limestone, polished and scalloped by the dissolving effect of acid waters from the fells above. The path is indistinct, so if it is misty take a compass bearing of 140 degrees for the next three-quarters of a mile (1.2km). The path becomes a double track further on. To the right is a row of cairns, with Pike Hill the most prominent. There are numerous shakeholes along the route, and several erratic blocks of gritstone on the limestone.

Following a shelf of the Main limestone, the route enters a wonderfully open and isolated piece of country, 'far from the madding crowd', where foxes roam and common violets push through the grass, where skylarks sing, kestrels hover and lapwings fall from the sky. Here is the haunt of the golden plover. The male's evocative note carries across the tussocks of grass. A short flight on long, narrow wings ends in a landing with wings held up before settling. These moorland birds breed in small colonies, preferring an area broken by low hummocks and ridges where the simple nests are well-hidden.

Just before a steep bank of white limestone, turn right towards the beckoning valley. Another right turn brings the path below the impressive limestone scar and scree of High Clint, while on the right is a limekiln. There is a good view of the meandering Ure in the valley below, and Dodd Fell straight across. Pass through a gate, turn right by a small wood of deciduous trees and down a long pasture to Shutt Lane.

Turn right down the lane between well-built sandstone walls to Sedbusk. This quiet, compact hamlet of farms and cottages on the 950 foot (300m) contour looks across Wensleydale to Hawes and Gayle. Turn right along the lane towards Simonstone, part of Lady Anne Clifford's Way, then down through the fields to the road. By the field gate on the road verge, look out for the delicate flowers of pink purslane, not a common flower. It has fleshy, hairless, bright green leaves, and veins of deeper colour on the five petals. You may also see it in Cotterdale village.

Cross the road and continue down to the packhorse bridge. At the road, go left over Haylands Bridge and along the riverbank, then through the fields on the flagstone-paved footpath into Hawes. On the left is the National Park information centre and the Dales Countryside Museum.

WALK 19: DODD FELL FROM GAYLE

Start: Gayle. Grid Ref: 871 892
Distance: 9 miles (14½ km)
OS Maps: Outdoor Leisure 2 or Landranger 98
Walking Time: 4½ hours

The main aim of this walk is to climb Dodd Fell, 1,500 feet (450m) above Gayle. It involves two ancient tracks. After a fairly gentle climb up the Cam Road, the path joins the Pennine Way with a short detour to the top, from where there are panoramic views

The quaint village of Gayle lies only a few hundred yards through the fields from Hawes, yet its history goes back a lot further in time. Flints found here suggest there was an Iron Age settlement, but Gayle itself began as a Viking summer farm. The Old Hall has a lintel dated 1695, though most of the houses are eighteenth or nineteenth century. Gayle Beck runs and tumbles in little waterfalls over solid limestone slabs through the heart of the village. Ducks and geese dabble in the

water, and houses and cottages look on. A stone bridge crosses the beck, below which is Gayle Mill.

Gayle was an important centre for the hand-knitting industry, where both women and men, old and young, using knitting sticks, belt and curved needles made stockings, hats and sailors' jerseys. They were poor people and poorly paid, taking their goods to the mill where machines, powered by the beck, spun the yarn. Gayle Mill was built in 1784, a fine three storey

Gayle.

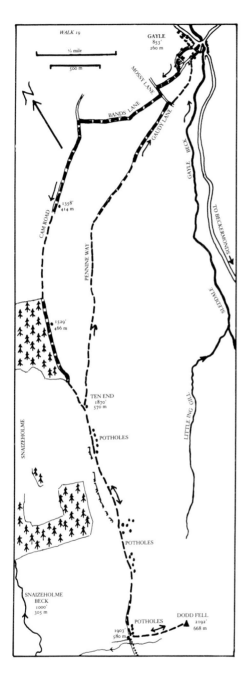

WALK 19

GAYLE
853'
260 m

¼ mile

500 m

MOSSY LANE

BANDS LANE

GAUDY LANE

GAYLE BECK

TO BECKERMONDS

1358'
414 m

CAM ROAD

PENNINE WAY

SLEDDALE

1529'
466 m

TEN END
1870'
570 m

LITTLE ING GILL

POTHOLES

SNAIZEHOLME

POTHOLES

SNAIZEHOLME
BECK
1000'
305 m

POTHOLES
1903'
580 m

DODD FELL
2192'
668 m

building which is little changed today. Some of the bigger houses in the village were used for woolcombing. Although the mill ceased as a woollen mill about 1850, the tradition of hand-knitting continued well into the twentieth century. By 1917, the water power of the mill was producing electricity and gave early electric street lighting to the village.

From the bridge, turn left past the Methodist church and further on past the Country Hotel. Turn right at the t-junction at the top of the village, climbing slowly, left at the next t-junction, then right past Low Bands and High Bands farms. On the grass verge in the summer grow the purple flowers of devilsbit scabious, the yellow, branched nipplewort, hawkweeds, may-weeds and goosegrass, visited by green-veined white and small tortoiseshell butterflies.

At the end of Bands Lane, proceed left onto the Cam Road. This is an old drove road over to Horton-in-Ribblesdale from Hawes. Such roads grew in importance when towns began to grow in the sixteenth century and larger meat supplies were needed. Drove roads became part of the road network, and drovers became so numerous that they were licensed. In *Roads and Trackways of the Yorkshire Dales*, Geoffrey Wright describes how the drover became so important that he was trusted to take money for wealthy merchants who wanted to pay a bill in another town. Instead of taking the gold, of which he could be robbed, the drover left the money at home and paid the sum from the sale of cattle ('gold on the hoof'). In time came the use of promissory notes, which bore the words 'I promise to pay the bearer . . .' – and this was the the forerunner of the banknote.

A stile and a field of ragwort on the Pennine Way near Gayle.

The track climbs to a higher level, over-looking Snaizeholme and Widdale, where patches of coniferous plantations cover the valley side. The track's cobbled surface is easy going, and it soon begins to get steeper alongside a conifer wood and a walled lane again. In the road there are ripple-marked slabs of stone, some with black (carbonised) plant remains. Above the plantation, near Ten End, the path is on the Main limestone with big slabs of beautifully-weathered fossil crinoids.

The route joins the Pennine Way at a cairn at Ten End. The Pennine Way was the first long-distance right of way in Britain. It was the inspiration and effort of Tom Stephenson, who as long ago as 1935 initiated the idea, and he was the true founder of this imaginative long-distance footpath for walkers across half of England. After many problems and difficulties came the approval of Parliament in 1951, but it wasn't until 1965 that all sections of the route were made legally passable and it was opened to the public.

There are exceptional views of the bowl-shaped end of the dale of Snaizeholme to the right and, down below, five or six farms (some now used as holiday cottages) and a small stretch of water in this deep, isolated valley where sheep and wildlife are little disturbed. Beyond the head of the Snaize-holme valley loom the distant shapes of Ingleborough and Whernside. The Pennine Way follows a terrace formed by the Main limestone. But soon the limestone wall turns to a gritstone one. Then, just where the first wall climbs up from the valley bottom on the right, turn off up the fellside to the left and make a bee-line for the top, a third of a mile (500m) away and 300 feet (90m) of ascent. Walkers are reminded that the steep climb to the top of Dodd Fell is not a public right of way and care should be taken to avoid damage to vegetation.

The pathless way is among cotton-grass, bilberry, peat and mat grass. You will also find cloudberry near the top, with its bright green leaves and occasional white flowers which turn to a yellow fruit in the autumn. A trig point crowns the summit, from which there is an all-round panorama of distant hills and mountains, including all of the Three Peaks, and a good view of Hawes, Gayle and the length of Wensleydale.

Return by the same route to the Pennine Way, turn right and go along it to the cairn where the path forks at Ten End peat grounds. Take the right fork, and the path follows the ridge and descends gradually to Gaudy Lane and to Gayle. Peat cutting was an annual toil for Dalesfolk, many of whom had rights of turbury, which allowed them to cut peat for their own use from common land on the fell. Cut in the spring, the peat was stacked to dry and brought down in the autumn using a coup, a broad sledge on metal runners pulled by a horse. A peat coup and some of the implements used in peat-cutting can be seen in the museum at Hawes. The valley on the right is Sleddale, in which Gayle Beck runs over Aysgill Force, one of the prettiest of waterfalls, reached by footpath from Gayle village.

WALK 20: COTTERDALE AND GREAT SHUNNER FELL

Start: Hardraw. Grid Ref: 867 912
Distance: 9½ miles (15km)
OS Maps: Pathfinder 608 or Landranger 98
Walking Time: 4½ hours

Great Shunner Fell is the highest point in Wensleydale, which makes a worthy goal for this energetic walk. From Hardraw it visits the pretty valley and village of Cotterdale, then climbs up through the forest, past the old coal pits, and up to the summit ridge. From the top there is a panoramic view. The return route follows the Pennine Way back to Hardraw. In places it is steep, wet or rough. Parking is limited to the roadside on the east side of Hardraw village.

Hardraw village lies across the River from Hawes and is one of a line of hamlets and villages like Simonstone, Sedbusk, Grange and Askrigg which lie at the foot of the fells on the north side of the dale. The name Hardraw means 'shepherd's dwelling' and sheep farming is as important as ever on the broad fells of Abbotside Common. There is the chuch, built in 1880, the old village school, a shop, cafe and the Green Dragon Inn; few of the houses are very old.

From the west end of the village, turn up the cobbled green lane to Cotterdale, past a building with its west wall clad in purple Welsh slate. The flower-bordered lane curves to the left and up the hill. The goldfinch is often seen near to the village, where there are plenty of weed seeds. A group of goldfinches is given the pleasant name of a 'charm'.

After a mile (1½km), the walled lane comes to an end at a gate and the path divides into three. The one on the right goes along the Hearne road to the old coal pits of Fossdale Moss. This track was in heavy use at the beginning of the twentieth century, when farmers still trundled their carts along it for a load of coal. Now it starts off well, but is so overgrown further along that it becomes difficult to follow and the going is rough. The centre path is our

return route from the top of Great Shunner Fell, the much-used Pennine Way. We take the left path, barely visible through the tufts of grass, to a wall which further along is crossed by a ladder stile.

From here is a fine view of upper Wensleydale between Widdale Fell and the sharp edge of Cotter End. The path descends gently to the right, and from the first gate there is a view into Cotterdale – the name refers to both the dale and the small village. The path passes through a series of stiles, past two barns and a small field kiln. Cotterdale Beck meanders idly along on the valley floor, unaware that it is going to plunge very soon over Cotter Force. Wheatears and whinchats are summer visitors to this hillside. The wheatear has an eye-catching white rump and moves frequently from one place to another, flying low to a rock, molehill or wall top, always restless with much bobbing and tail fanning. The whinchat is also easily seen as it perches in a prominent place to deliver its jingling song. Perhaps its most distinguishing feature is the white stripe, or supercilium, above the eye.

Cotterdale is a most peaceful valley, and the little hamlet seems quite remote and part of another age. A survey of 1603 shows six titled or wealthy men lived here, and three centuries later the names of three

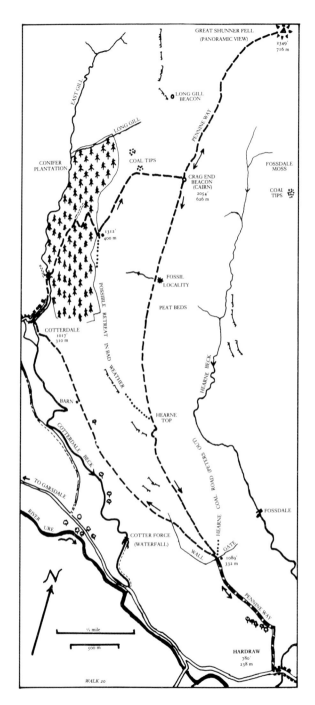

GREAT SHUNNER FELL
(PANORAMIC VIEW)
2349'
716 m

LONG GILL
BEACON

EAST GILL

LONG GILL

PENNINE WAY

CONIFER
PLANTATION

COAL TIPS

CRAG END
BEACON
(CAIRN)
2054'
626 m

FOSSDALE
MOSS

COAL
TIPS

1312'
400 m

FOSSIL
LOCALITY

PEAT BEDS

POSSIBLE RETREAT IN BAD WEATHER

COTTERDALE
1017'
310 m

HEARNE BECK

BARN

COTTERDALE BECK

HEARNE
TOP

HEARNE COAL ROAD (PETERS OUT)

TO GARSDALE

FOSSDALE

RIVER URE

COTTER FORCE
(WATERFALL)

WALL

GATE

1089'
332 m

PENNINE WAY

½ mile

500 m

HARDRAW
780'
238 m

WALK 20

Field barns in Cotterdale.

families were used in a rhyme: 'Three Halls, two Kirks and a King. Same road out as goes in'. There are farms and cottages, some of which were colliers' homes when the pits were working and when most of the women did hand-knitting to trade in Hawes. The small Methodist chapel is now a private house, but still has one or two gravestones in the garden. A shepherd's cottage is dated 1616.

Just below the village, the two streams of East Gill and West Gill meet to become Cotterdale Beck. Pass the ford and the houses which face East Gill, keeping to the left bank, and cross the beck by the footbridge. A small path leads up through the trees and brings you out onto a forest road. There is plenty of interest for the botanist in Cotterdale and varieties of orchid are worth looking out for. The forest

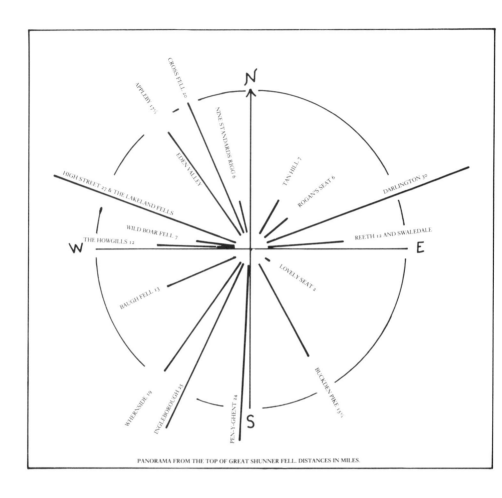

is mainly spruce and managed by the Economic Forestry Group.

After about three-quarters of a mile (1.2km) don't miss the turn up to the right. The track, covered with buttercups and daisies, zigzags through the conifers to emerge on the edge of the fell. To the right is a bridleway back to Hardraw, a possible retreat in poor weather. Turn left to the Cotterdale coal pits. Notice the tall beacon of Long Gill on the horizon and the cairn on the right. It is the cairn that you must

aim for later. The track curves to the right and peters out among the spoil heaps, where you can still pick up small lumps of coal. The coal seam is the Tan Hill Coal, which further north reaches a maximum thickness of three feet six inches (1.1m).

From the coal pits, make for the cairn on the horizon (not always visible) straight up onto the shoulder of Shunner Fell and the line of the Pennine Way. The cairn is named Crag End Beacon and the original structure is now just a pile of stones. From it you can see the summit cairn and over to the right a small forest of beacons. It has been suggested that during the Scottish raids such beacons were built to look like armies of Yorkshiremen ready to fend off any attack! Among the moorland birds is the golden plover, and you may also hear or see the skylark, curlew, meadow pipit and kestrel. The short-eared owl frequents the Pennine Way in the early morning, before the walkers arrive.

It is just over a mile to the top (1.8km), and a little way up the track the bright little flowers of water crowfoot grow in a watery hollow in the peat. The walk to the top is exhilarating, and at an altitude of 2,340 feet (716m) the summit of Great Shunner Fell is the highest point in Wensleydale. The triangulation pillar is built of stone rather than the usual concrete and the view from it is quite magnificent. To the west, the Lake District hills are visible, with the Howgills in the middle distance. To the right of the Eden Valley is the scarp edge of the Pennines, with Cross Fell the highest point. Nine Standards Rigg lies six miles (9 km) to the north, and the road up to Tan Hill can be seen to the right of it. You can see into Swaledale, though a better view can be obtained by walking another half mile (800m) along the ridge. Lovely Seat is only two miles (3km) away, then Buckden Pike, and the Three Peaks – Pen-y-ghent,

Ingleborough and Whernside – lie to the south.

Follow the well-marked route of the Pennine Way all the way down to Hardraw. First, retrace your steps to Crag End Beacon then, after crossing a boggy area and just before the peat hags, look out for chunks of whitish rock to the right of the path. (A streamlet and small gully starts down to the right from this point.) The rock looks rather like a limestone pavement, but is in fact is a pure quartz rock known as gannister. It contains wonderful examples of the fossil root *Stigmaria*. They are covered with rootlets which leave rows of dots, and the rootlets can be seen in section, penetrating through the rock. Gannister is extremely hard and represents a fossil soil where everything has been washed out of it, leaving pure silica sand. These roots belonged to coal forest trees which form a thin coal seam above the gannister.

Pass the peat hags, through the cotton grass and mat grass, an area of old coal pits (the Tan Hill coal again) and through the millstone grit (notice the white quartz pebbles in the rock); then through the beds of limestone and chert (evidence of quarrying) down to the walled lane. This is where you rejoin the route which began the walk and returns you to Hardraw village.

WALK 21: HELL GILL FROM APPERSETT

Start: Appersett. Grid Ref: 859 907
Distance: 14 miles (22km)
OS Maps: Pathfinder 608 and 617, or Landranger 98
Walking Time: 6½ hours

This is a superb walk almost to the source of the River Ure. Allow plenty of time because it is fairly long. First a low route visits Mossdale Head, Blades and Lunds Church, before climbing to Hell Gill and the border with Cumbria. The high level return explores a section of Lady Anne Clifford's Way, with fine views, and descends from Cotter End back to Appersett. Paths are good for the most part. There is limited parking by the green in Appersett.

By the bridge over Widdale Beck lies Appersett, the first village of Wensleydale. Like several other places ending in 'sett', it was named as a summer farm or *saetr* by the Norse settlers. Most of the placenames in the upper dale are of Norse origin, and include Birkrigg, Mossdale, Thwaite, Lunds and Hell Gill itself. Divided by the main road, the village has a green decorated with geese, goats and washing lines, and the cottages look the other way. The broad beck doubles as a duck pond. But although it has good communications on a crossing of routes, from Wensleydale to Garsdale and from Ribblehead to Swaledale, Appersett seems a sleepy place and visitors often pass through.

Start by crossing the bridge over Widdale Beck, past a well-preserved limekiln. Take the field path, which goes alongside the road to New Bridge over the Ure, then up the left side of the river. There are woods along its banks, with birch, beech, oak, rowan, alder and sycamore. The common alder is typical of the water's edge and may be recognised at any season be the small, dark, oval cones. This small tree has a conical shape and is most valuable in conserving banks of rivers and streams.

Two-thirds of a mile (1km) from New Bridge, take the ladder stile on the right through the woods to Birkrigg Farm.

Across on the other side of the river is the pretty waterfall of Cotterdale Force, reached from the road.

Pass Birkrigg Farm on the left and go along Hollin Bank. In the early summer the flowers here are amazing. Purple betony and foxglove line the path. Lovely ragged robin and sweet woodruff grow in a wet spot, then there is a flowery field with hawkweed, clovers, forget-me-not, oxeye daisy and yarrow. In the next wet place grows the bright yellow monkeyflower, and further along greater knapweed, meadowsweet and wood cranesbill.

Rejoin the river, keeping on the same side as you come to Mossdale Beck. At Mossdale Head, go in front of the farmhouse and round the barn to the small bridge over the beck. The old railway to Garsdale crossed Mossdale Gill by a viaduct, and views from the train must have been breathtaking. For the walker today there is a picturesque view of the waterfalls with the railway arches in the background. Mossdale is the smallest side dale and there is another waterfall higher up. The beck comes down from Widdale Fell, the highest point of which at 2,203 feet (672m) is called Great Knoutberry Hill.

From the little bridge, go straight across, up along a broken wall and turn right through a gap, descending to a wall and to the road at Thwaite Bridge House. A footpath goes over to Cotterdale from here, but take the one across the river and to the left through double gates signposted 'Yore House 1½'. The land soon becomes poor, and although partridge find cover in the bits of scattered woodland, the meadow pipit, skylark and wheatear are common on the rough grazing land. You will hear the call of the curlew too, its liquid, bubbling song being confined to the breeding season. The young River Ure is a mere beck as it meanders through the drumlins. Opposite Yore House is the Moorcock Inn, at the junction of roads and near to Garsdale Head station on the Settle-Carlisle railway. It is a wild and windy place, and the inn has provided shelter and warmth to many travellers over the years.

Our route reaches Blades, which makes a good stopping place, and where afternoon teas are served as well as various beers. To continue, go round the back of the buildings, through two gates and make for the white footbridge, then turn right then left alongside a small plantation. The path carries on through two white gates and over a rounded hill (a drumlin), a relic of the Ice Age, called Cowshaw, from the top of which several more examples can be seen as well as Lunds Church below on the right. There are no villages in these parts. Farms are distanced from each other in high and difficult country, which lies well over 1,000 feet (300m) above sea level, and there are Norse names like Lunds, Shaws and Beckside which tell of the first settlers. It is possible that the Norse language was still heard in these parts until the sixteenth century, and the Yorkshire dialect owes much to Norse influence. The isolation is emphasised by the little chapel of Lunds and its graveyard, far from the road. The church is probably late seventeenth century and its simplicity suggests it was built by the parishoners themselves. It is said that

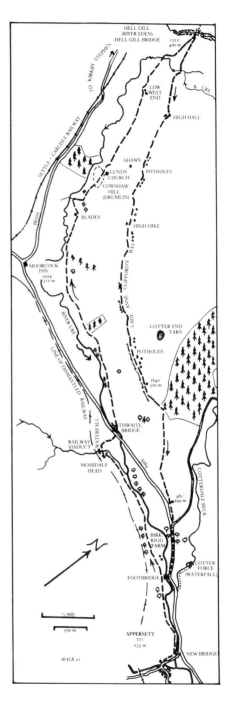

Lunds Church, the River Ure and Wild Boar Fell.

before the church was built, services were held on the top of Cowshaw hill and people were called by the beating of an iron pan. For nearly forty years Rev Pinck, the intrepid Vicar of Hardraw, walked the 5½ miles (9km) each Sunday for the service at Lunds. One snowy day when crossing a gully he missed the stone slab bridge, sank into ten feet (3m) of soft snow and only just managed to get out. On another occasion after severe flooding, he had to crawl along the tops of walls to reach the church.

The path continues between the farm and barn of Beckside, and stays with the low route through flowery fields to the white farmhouse of Low West End among the trees. John Blades came from West End and, as a young man, went to London where he found a job as a errand boy to a glass merchant. He later married the daughter, inherited the ornamental cut glass business and in 1813 became the Sheriff of London.

Go down the farm road to the bridge but, before the bridge, turn right along a cart track, and keep straight on up the hillside. Cross a small beck – the River Ure! Bear right past a field kiln, then Jingling Hole, where a stream emerges on the left, and on up to Hell Gill Bridge. Hell Gill forms both the county boundary and that of the National Park. Dick Turpin is said to have escaped from Yorkshire when he leapt across the gorge of Hell Gill on horseback. The limestone gorge is so narrow in places that it is quite possible for an athletic man to jump across – but don't try it! From the bridge you get a downward glimpse of the forty foot (12m) deep canyon. The total length of the gorge is a third of a mile (500m), over fifty feet (15m) deep in places and, although the stream bed in the bottom widens out, the walls above narrow to three feet (1m) across. Wearing wetsuits, gorge-bashers start at the top, rock-hopping and scrambling down the steep ravine of falls and pools, jumping one steep waterfall into the deep plunge-pool below for a short swim, and marvelling at an underworld in semi-darkness. Walkers can explore a short way into the gorge from the upper or lower end without getting too wet, and share some of the wonder and excitement.

The bridge over the gill carried the highway from Hawes to Kirkby Stephen, and used to see a busy stream of traffic until 1825 when the new turnpike road – now the B6259 – was built lower down. The view ahead is into Mallerstangdale, with Wild Boar Fell rearing up to the left.

For the return route, retrace your steps for a few paces and fork left across some

Ring ouzel.

limestone pavements. A little to the left is Jingling Sike Cave, where the water disappears beneath the ground to join the infant Ure just above Green Bridge, 300 yards (275m) below. Between Hell Gill Bridge and Jingling Sike Cave you have crossed the main watershed of England. Hell Gill Beck joins the Eden and flows into the Irish Sea, and the River Ure joins the Ouse to flow into the North Sea.

Keep to the left of a walled pasture. Several becks cross the path, revealing limestone overlain by black shale. The scalloped surface of the limestone is brought about by the dissolving power of the acid waters that flow off the peaty fells. The shelter of the gills provides nesting places for the ring ouzel – often called the mountain blackbird. Listen for the clear ringing song, 'cheroo, cheroo cheri, ch-cho-oo', repeated a few times.

High Hall, formerly Highway House and now derelict, was an inn which once saw a good trade. Further along is High Dike, another abandoned building which was also an inn on this busy road. The landlords used to tell how the seventeenth century highwayman John Nevison often called here on his grey horse. Perhaps it was 'Swift Nick' who leapt Hell Gill?

The highway has seen important goods and historical figures pass by. The timber for the building of Bolton Castle came this way in the fourteenth century, and Mary Queen of Scots rode by in 1568 to be imprisoned in the same castle. In 1663, Lady Anne Clifford passed north with her retinue to Pendragon Castle in Mallerstangdale. And each autumn the road was particularly busy, with drovers bringing sheep, cattle and horses to the fairs in Wensleydale and Wharfedale.

The path descends for a mile (1½ km) from Cotter End to the main road, with good views of Cotterdale on the way down. Walk along the road for half a mile (800m) and turn right to the river, signed 'Appersett'. This last section is the same as the first part of the walk.

.

SELECTED READING

General:
Arthur Raistrick, *The Pennine Dales* (Eyre and Spottiswoode, 1968). A broad look at the Yorkshire Dales, the geology, prehistory and historical development.
Tony Waltham, *Yorkshire Dales National Park* (Webb and Bower, 1987). The latest official guide to the National Park. Well-written and informative.
Geoffrey N Wright, *The Yorkshire Dales* (David and Charles, 1986). Informative on natural history, history, mining and quarrying. Includes a gazetteer.
Marie Hartley and Joan Ingilby, *The Yorkshire Dales* (Dent, 1956; reprinted by Smith Settle, 1991). A compact description of all the dales.
R W Morris, *Yorkshire through Place Names* (David and Charles, 1982). Relates settlement and place names to the geography and geology.
Alan Kind (ed), *Wensleydale and Upper Wharfedale* (David and Charles, 1990). A general guide for use with OS Landranger map 98.

Geology:
Arthur Raistrick and John L Illingworth, *The Face of North West Yorkshire* (Dalesman, 1959). A background to geology and natural vegetation.
Derek Brumhead, *Geology Explained in the Yorkshire Dales and on the Yorkshire Coast* (David and Charles, 1979). Contains an itinerary for Mill Gill.
K C Dunham and A A Wilson, *Geology of the Northern Pennine Orefield, Vol 2* (British Geological Survey, 1985). Very detailed Dales geology.

History:
Harry Speight, *Romantic Richmondshire* (Elliot Stock, 1897). A reliable history of Wensleydale and Swaledale.
Patricia Dingwall, *Wensleydale* (Discovery Guides Ltd, 1989). A brief summary of history and places to visit.
Ella Pontefract and Marie Hartley, *Wensleydale* (Dent, 1936; reprinted Smith Settle, 1988). Covers the whole dale with many delightful stories.
Marie Hartley and Joan Ingilby, *Yorkshire Village* (Dent, 1953; reprinted Smith Settle, 1989). A classic history of Askrigg.
Peter Gunn, *The Yorkshire Dales. Landscape with Figures* (Century Publishing, 1984). Contains a chapter on historic Middleham.
Arthur Raistrick, *Pennine Walls* (Dalesman, 1988). Who built them, why and how.
Susan D Brooks, *Parish and People of the Yorkshire Dales through ten Centuries.* (Published by the author, 1973). The Church and its effect on local life.
C S Hallas, *The Wensleydale Railway* (Dalesman, 1984).
David Hall, *Burtersett Quarries. A Wensleydale Mining Community.* (Published by the author, 1985).
Geoffrey N Wright, *Roads and Trackways of the Yorkshire Dales* (Moorland Publishing, 1985). A new and attractive study of a little recorded subject.

124

Marie Hartley and Joan Ingilby, *The Old Hand-knitters of the Dales* (Dent, 1951; fourth edition by Dalesman, 1988).
John Waddington-Feather, *Yorkshire Dialect* (Dalesman, 1970).

Natural History:
W R Mitchell and R W Robson, *Pennine Birds* (Dalesman, 1973). Useful for birds of the uplands.
J Ferguson-Lees (*et al*), *The Shell Guide to the Birds of Britain and Ireland* (Michael Joseph, 1983). One of the best general bird books.

Deborah Millward, *Flora of Wensleydale* (Yordale Natural History Society, 1988). Contains a useful landform map and notes on geology, climate and soils of the dale by Professor C A M King.
Sylvia Arnold, *Wild Flowers of the Yorkshire Dales* (Hutton, 1988).
Joan E Duncan and R W Robson, *Pennine Flowers* (Dalesman, 1977). Flowers of the uplands with a section on plant lore.
Franklyn Perring, *RSNC Guide to British Wild Flowers* (Country Life Books, 1984). Very useful for learning common species and sorting out 'look-alikes'.
M J Delany (ed), *Yorkshire Mammals* (University of Bradford, 1985). Detailed description of species with useful distribution maps

Walking:
Mike Harding, *Walking the Dales* (Michael Joseph, 1986). Includes three walks in Wensley-dale.
Colin Speakman, *Walking in the Yorkshire Dales* (Hale, 1982). A comprehensive and authoritative guide.

INDEX

Illustrations are numbered in italics